PANDEMONIUM

Also by Luuk van Middelaar and published by Agenda

Alarums and Excursions:
Improvising Politics on the European Stage

PANDEMONIUM

Saving Europe

LUUK VAN MIDDELAAR

Translated by Liz Waters

agenda
publishing

English translation © Agenda Publishing Ltd

Translated by Liz Waters

First published as *Een Europees pandemonium. Kwetsbaarheid en politieke kracht* by Historische Uitgeverij, Groningen

© Luuk van Middelaar 2021

This publication has been made possible with financial support from the Dutch Foundation for Literature.

Nederlands
letterenfonds
dutch foundation
for literature

Agenda Publishing Ltd
The Core
Bath Lane
Newcastle Helix
Newcastle upon Tyne
NE4 5TF

www.agendapub.com

ISBN 978-1-78821-423-0

British Library Cataloguing-in-Publication Data
A catalogue record for this book is
available from the British Library

Typeset by Patty Rennie
Printed and bound in the UK by TJ Books

Contents

Acknowledgements

This book's elucidation of the European response to the coronavirus crisis is based almost entirely on published sources. Nevertheless, it could not have been written but for highly productive exchanges with friends and others backstage in Berlin, Brussels, The Hague, Frankfurt, Paris and Rome. I would like to express my heartfelt thanks to all of them.

A special word of thanks to Hans Kribbe, as well as to Monika Sie Dhian Ho and Frans-Paul van der Putten for the (geo-)political insights derived from our conversations; to my publishers and editors Patrick Everard (Historische Uitgeverij), Heinrich Geiselberger (Suhrkamp Verlag) and Alison Howson (Agenda Publishing) for their stimulation and sharp observations; to translator Liz Waters for her steadfast feeling for language; and to Manon de Boer and Julius for their invigorating company in the year of the pandemic.

LvM

21 May 2021

Prologue: panic

All were attacked, although all did not die.

Jean de la Fontaine,
"The Animals Sick of the Plague"

The cry of despair grows louder. In the final winter weeks of 2020, an insidious virus seeds itself across an inattentive continent, pitching tens of thousands into a life-and-death battle. Most European states secure their borders, millions of households lock their front doors, while day after day television news programmes tally the dead and honour doctors and nurses as if they were soldiers going off to war. Military columns bearing Lombardy's Covid coffins; abandoned and lifeless Madrid care homes; mobile crematoria in Wuhan: hellish scenes flash by, feeding fears of social contact and infection. In Europe a disaster is unfolding, but there is no joint response. No action.

The loudest cry comes from Italy, hit by the virus early on. Appeals for help go unanswered and bitter reproaches ensue. "If in this hour of truth we receive no support, then we're better off outside the Union", is the sentiment, echoed, if less shrilly, in Spain. Elsewhere too, the slow, feeble reaction of the European institutions contrasts starkly with the

1

personal tragedies in hospitals and care homes from Bergamo to Madrid, Mulhouse or Tilburg. The hastily closed internal borders are regarded as another scandal. If the Union cannot guarantee freedom of movement, its biggest boast for so many years, if freedom of movement actually becomes a source of danger, then irrelevance and implosion threaten.

It is striking how quickly the concerns and admonitions are transformed into doubts about the survival of the European Union itself. All over the world the unknowns of the coronavirus are demanding the utmost of leaders and populations. The speed of its spread, epidemiological uncertainty and social confusion put all political systems to the test. In China Covid-19 shines a light on the weaknesses and strengths of an authoritarian state. After an embarrassing phase of denial and censorship, Xi's government deals resolutely with the calamity. In the United States the pandemic makes a fool of the president, an impulsive leader in a time of crisis, as within sight of an election he zigzags between the obscenity of hundreds of thousands of deaths and the price of a lockdown. Yet no one concludes that either country might fall apart as a result of the virus. For the Union, by contrast, the crisis is instantly, as if automatically, seen as a threat to its very existence.

Amid the pandemic clamour about the approaching end of Europe, two choruses can be heard. First there are the voices of conscience. On Easter Sunday, from a practically empty St Peter's Basilica in Rome, Pope Francis addresses the city and the world. Recalling the devastation and reconstruction after 1945, he pleads with his listeners: "It is more urgent than ever that rivalries do not regain force, but that all recognize themselves as part of a single family and support one another".[1] A few days later, a Luxembourg cardinal speaks of "disenchantment" with the European project, saying the virus might prove its "fatal wound".[2] In late March, Jacques Delors, former president of the European Commission, senses in the lack of solidarity between the nations a "deadly danger" for the Union. The 94-year-old says sombrely, embracing the metaphor, "the microbe is back".[3] A similar message comes from Jean-Claude Juncker, one of Delors' successors, in an Austrian newspaper: "the European spirit is in danger".[4] Figures of moral and political authority lay the stress on Europe as a spiritual project, on a community of destiny that should transcend national egotism. In the absence of solidarity, Europe as an idea will die.

Then there are the disconcerted voices of finance, sounding from London, New York and Frankfurt. Fearing Europe's demise as a currency and a market, they recall the breathtaking financial and economic crises the monetary union passed through from 2008 onwards. Mario Draghi, former president of the European Central Bank, warns of a "human tragedy of potentially biblical proportions".[5] Doubts among investors about the solvency of the Italian government might trigger a euro crisis, is one fear voiced in the *Financial Times*.[6] Employers share that concern. On British television the Italian premier Giuseppe Conte characterizes the socio-economic consequences of the pandemic as "a big challenge to the existence of Europe", warning that the risk of its collapse is "real".[7] In dry, official tones, the services of the Commission report in early May that "there is a risk that the crisis could lead to severe distortions within the Single Market and to entrenched economic, financial and social divergences between euro area Member States".[8] It seems the intricate economic fabric woven between the member states that makes the Union so robust is about to unravel.

Outside voices too predict the end of Europe. Not in the tragic language of concern, warning or evocation, but in cutting, mocking, sneering tones, whipped up by Beijing and Moscow: taunts, provocation, even delight. For them the announcement of Europe's death is not a tragedy but an opportunity, an event in an epic with a different protagonist. To anyone willing to listen, they gibe that Brussels is suddenly absent and that you would do better to turn to China or Russia for a shipping container of face masks, since times of need tell you who your friends are. The Chinese ambassador in Paris scoffs that "the staff of old folk's homes have deserted their posts en masse from one day to the next, abandoning residents to hunger, sickness and death".[9] A Russian senator spreads a false report that the Polish government has denied Russian aircraft carrying emergency medical aid destined for Italy access to its airspace.[10] Its enemies smile derisively at European division, at the helplessness of the open society, and brandish the enticements of the strong state, with its unity and discipline.

Amid this anguished tumult, against most expectations and therefore practically unnoticed, the Union, in the midst of the pandemic and very quickly, draws itself up to its full height. A few firm political decisions belie all the fatalism. By Maundy Thursday on 9 April 2020 – three days before the papal appeal from St Peter's – European finance ministers have averted the acute financial threat. On 18 May, three days before Ascension, the German chancellor and the French president reaffirm their desire for a common future in Europe, as Europe. Like true time-artists, they convert the perilous moment into a passage, a transition in time toward a new chosen future.

But what remains, above all in Italy, is the memory of failure at a moment of truth. It creates doubt about Europe's capacity to survive the pandemic shocks and economic turbulence as a unity, all the more so since no one has forgotten how the Union fell short on several occasions during the past decade. Time and again, Europe's end was announced, although it never arrived. How should we interpret this uncertainty and vulnerability? Is there no self-assurance to be derived from the experience of earlier crises? Does Europe not prove itself able each time to hold crises in check, demonstrating unexpected resilience?

"Pandemonium" is the capital city of hell in Milton's *Paradise Lost*, where demons rule the roost amid a wild chaos of tumult and screams. A pandemic is no pandemonium, but during this pandemic the false prophets dance around the fire of confusion, the lamentation of imperilled souls combines with the cries of the sick and the sighs of the dying, while Covid devils set breathless bodies against one another, sow discord over the constraints placed on the healthy and provoke resentment of those to blame for this descent into the inferno.

Yet like earlier great events, this ordeal will have a purifying effect, not least because of the public commotion it causes in the Union. In the pandemic hullabaloo lie not only discord and strife but the surprise of a shared experience, the discovery that, with paradise lost, there is a prize to be won, a shared place in time.

> And not worrying about taking any rest, we mounted
> up, he first and I second, so that I saw some of the lovely
> things that are in the heavens, through a round opening;
> and then we emerged to see the stars again.[11]

1

The experience of a crisis

Nay, some were so enthusiastically bold as to run about the streets with their oral predictions, pretending they were sent to preach to the city; and one in particular, who, like Jonah to Nineveh, cried in the streets, "Yet forty days, and London shall be destroyed".

Daniel Defoe, *A Journal of the Plague Year*[1]

A series of escapes

For more than a decade, European states and societies had been rocked by severe disruption. Unprepared, unprotected, they withstood it as best they could.

Four acute crises caught the collaborative venture off guard: the banking and euro crisis (2008–12), the Ukraine crisis (2014–15), the migrant crisis (2015–16) and the Atlantic crisis of Brexit-&-Trump (2016–20). Four times the patiently constructed decision-making factory that served the market, the currency and freedom of movement was pummelled by divisive forces. Four times government leaders, ministers, commissioners and central bankers hurried to Brussels, Luxembourg or Frankfurt for "last chance" consultations, in which they reshaped the European Union. Four times too, all across

Europe, a polyphonic public climbed onto its seats to jeer or applaud, occupied squares, waved flags and won back the power of the ballot box in renewed, intense engagement with the political drama taking place on the European stage.

Riding the waves of each crisis, prophets of doom announced the end of the Union. The most eager among them provided a date. "In a matter of months" the euro might well be finished, predicted top economist Paul Krugman in May 2012, while his colleague Willem Buiter spoke of "weeks, it could be days".[2] In early 2016, when one European internal border after another was shut in response to chaos on the external borders, Commission president Juncker imagined in his New Year press conference the end of Schengen, the internal market, the euro.[3] After a majority of British voters decided in June that year to leave the Union – and even more so when, the following November, American voters elected Donald Trump president – many were again certain that the hour had come. Member states would fall like dominoes – Brexit Nexit Frexit – until no Union remained.

Yet the European Union survived those four formidable crises. The euro is still with us. How come? Observers always underestimate the invisible glue that holds the club together. It consists in the first instance of a ubiquitous interweaving of economic interests between member states, for which the founders created the frameworks in 1950, configured by millions of moves, initiatives, and transactions by cross-border citizens and companies. Tearing that fabric apart would be costly (as the voices of finance know perfectly well). But that is not all. Critics repeatedly fail to appreciate the powerful political will, grounded in history, in Paris and Berlin in particular, to build a common European future. When it was a matter of whether to eject Greece from the currency union, that country was saved not to prevent financial loss but to head off graver political dangers – threats to the stability of the country and of the Balkans; threats to the Franco-German friendship and to Europe's standing in the world. When Russia menaced the continental order of states by intervening in Ukraine, and even shot down a passenger plane, all members reconciled themselves to the harmful effects of economic sanctions in order to exert pressure on the Kremlin as a unified bloc. When the authorities came close to losing control in the refugee crisis, the Union was prepared to act out of character and strike a deal with Turkey that would, at least, make the situation on its south-eastern external border manageable. Even the message from British Leave voters has at last been understood: the Union, long praised and reviled for the economic freedoms it created, must now urgently protect citizens, their jobs, their environment, their territory. The response beat back the electoral assault upon Europe from the spring of 2017 onwards – beginning in France and the Netherlands. Naturally such dénouements, interpreted as death-defying escapes, hold no guarantees for the future. Scars remain. Yet the Union undeniably evinces a robust vitality.

The immediate panic of the first coronavirus months in 2020 quickly swelled into a state of total crisis. Memories of how recent tribulations panned out did not inspire confidence, in fact they acted as salt in the wounds. Was the shortage of beds in Italian intensive care units not the consequence of the heartless cuts imposed by Brussels during the euro crisis? Was the closing of borders against the spread of the virus not a repeat of the national egotism seen in the refugee crisis? Even the Brexit episode, which reached its conclusion shortly before the Covid crisis with the official departure of the UK on 31 January 2020, could be heard echoing through the first wave of the pandemic; when premier Boris Johnson came down with a bad case of Covid-19, the tabloid press in London had no hesitation in blaming his team's contacts with EU negotiator Michel Barnier, likewise felled by the virus. Experiences mount up, like layers of sediment over time.

Rhetoric of expectation

That a mood of panic can so easily and repeatedly take hold of Europe is due first of all to a lack of insight into the resilience of the pact and an underestimation of the metamorphosis that the Union is going through. Yet this is not a full explanation. No less essential in the crises is the rhetoric of hope and fear that attaches itself indissolubly – in all our societies' public lives – to political action.

We are familiar with rhetorical dramatization by doom merchants who play upon the fears of their audience. In that sense the pandemic is no different from the London plague of 1665–66, when astrological pamphlets about the end of time were in great demand, as Daniel Defoe reported in *A Journal of the Plague Year*.[4] But rhetorical dramatization is also an instrument of government, used to mobilize the support of the public and force hesitant players to act. Controlled panic can shake things up, focus minds or put opponents under pressure. It was the latter that French president Macron, for example, had in mind with his dramatic conclusion in the *Financial Times* in April 2020 that the "European adventure could be thrown into disarray should Germany and the Netherlands not quickly show solidarity with Southern Europe in the pandemic".[5]

Experience teaches that diverse interests within the Union rely on cries of distress to bring different parties into line. Only the threatened loss of the public good of European peace, openness and prosperity – in normal times invisible or taken for granted – is sufficient to get the main players to act. Unlike wishful doom-prophesy, governmental panic-rhetoric is a precursor to action. At the same time, the executive's need for a state of emergency reveals a fundamental weakness of the Union, namely its inability to anticipate, to act in a timely fashion to forestall a threat.

The warning needs to be well-timed too. In the euro crisis there were indeed moments, in May 2010 for example, when salvation could come only from rapid, binding decisions. Naked calculation of probability prompted the leaders to act, a chorus of catastrophists increased the urgency, while the public held its breath as it watched what looked like a game of chicken between markets and politicians, a test to see who would be first to succumb to fear.

Using an existential crisis as a threat is a risky game in itself. That too became clear in the euro crisis. The rules said that a local Greek fire could not be put out till it was in danger of setting all of Europe ablaze. From 2010 onwards, Athens was helped not for solidarity's sake, but – at the urging of Germany and the Netherlands – in order to guarantee the "financial stability" of the entire eurozone. Arguments for that approach drew on moral hazard (you do not want to encourage players to divest responsibility for fire prevention onto their neighbours), but that is pretty dangerous. You are, after all, playing with fire. It is also counter-intuitive; a fireman who manifestly keeps the hoses shut off will not reassure onlookers.

Rarely does a dynamic of frightening words and images have such a torrid effect as during the British referendum debate of 2016 about a future inside or outside the Union. To Remain voters, exit meant the country would fall straight into the abyss; reason enough for their campaign to be dismissed as Project Fear by their opponents.* The Leave camp also resorted to intimidation. As Johnson and Farage saw it, Brussels was prepared – mere months after the refugee crisis – to unleash an invasion of rapists and terrorists on the English coast.

The competitive anxiety game dismayed even J. K. Rowling, author of the Harry Potter novels. "I'm not an expert on much, but I do know how to create a monster", she wrote shortly before referendum day in Britain. Of course both sides were appealing to the "universal need to make sense of the world by storytelling", but in this case "they have not been afraid to conjure monsters calculated to stir up our deepest fears". The writer, who found the Brexit monsters rather "ugly", knew better than anyone that once they escaped from the imagination, they would go on to lead a life of their own.[6]

By the time the British decision to leave the EU finally became a practical reality at the start of 2021, there had been so many plot twists that the public could no longer judge which of the horror stories of 2016 were well founded and

---

* It is worth noting that the argument of peace (between the Republic of Ireland and Northern Ireland), the ultimate *raison d'être* of the European Union, was barely mentioned in the Remain campaign, although the Irish border issue later grew to become the biggest obstacle to an agreement on an orderly withdrawal of the UK from the Union and continues to haunt UK–EU relations.

which had been overblown. The pandemic was a very different story. Future expectations and coronavirus outcomes bit off each other's heads. The virus, a microscopic monster, began its treacherous work even before the spotlight was turned on it. Morbid scenes in hospital wards, dark uncertainties, a big jolt of panic – a great stage had already been erected on which tales of monsters, prophesies of doom, enforcement orders, hocus-pocus statistics, conspiracy theories and vaccine hopes all fought for the favours of the bewildered public.

In such a situation there is but a marginal distinction between raising false alarm and maintaining confidence, a fine line between doom-prophesy and governmental prudence. Political spectacle guaranteed.

When the curtain rises

Does the coronavirus mark the start of a new era? In March 2020, *New York Times* columnist Thomas Friedman boldly spoke of an historic divide between the world BC and AC: Before Corona and After Corona.[7] Covid-19 as the new year zero.

While it still dizzies us and we gasp for breath, the historical significance of the events that have overtaken us cannot be evaluated straight away. This is why Hegel's Owl of Minerva spreads her wings only with the onset of dusk. The pandemic of 2020 brings a caesura, an incision in time – that much is clear – but how "historic" is the break between before and after?

Of course the impact of events provides a benchmark. Take the financial earthquake of 15 September 2008. It had massive consequences, ushered in global economic catastrophe, decided the American presidential election (which Barack Obama won) and led to Europe's euro crisis. Yet it was only later that we realized "Lehman Brothers" was far bigger than we were capable of seeing at the moment the earthquake struck. The crisis fed disillusionment among American voters about globalization, put an end to China's respect for the West's political proficiency and economic ingenuity, and created the conditions for the election of Donald Trump eight years later. So over time the event increased in size. How will it be with the pandemic? Will that too acquire the status of a divide between epochs, or rapidly shrink in the public memory? The historians who come after us will know better than we do. Yet given the magnitude and radical nature of the events and reactions, the speed and global extent of the spread of the virus, and immense shifts in the political forcefield, there is every reason to try to untangle and interpret the pandemonium.

Events do not just cut time into a before and after, they reveal something about the present. It is precisely in this sense that the coronavirus pandemic stands out, as astute interpreters realized at once.[8] Hidden weaknesses come to light, slow trends may be caught in the moment. This can be seen on a small scale, as the virus – spitefully – thrusts vulnerable citizens into a life-and-death battle. It can also be seen on a large scale, in organizations, businesses or countries that find themselves in dire straits as a consequence of their public health response. On the world stage too, the virus is a great revealer. America's involvement with the rest of the world is declining by fits and starts, China's hegemony is making itself felt and Europe is being forced to redefine its geopolitical position.

It is easy to assert that the coronavirus has exposed reality, but harder to determine which changes will be permanent, which shifts will be given a decisive nudge, which innovations would not have occurred without the pandemic. That is the intention of this book. Weighing up the impact of the virus on the Union will clarify and deepen our insight into role changes and turns of plot in Europe's political theatre.

The crisis, after all, presents a magnified picture of the strengths and weaknesses of European politics, of moods, motives, powers, forms and layers of time in the Union. In essence, politics revolves around our collective dealings with contingency, our joint approach to the vicissitudes of fate. So a crisis reveals how a system responds, what it can do, who takes the lead, which leadership style convinces the public, where the stuff of conflict and counterforces lies, how a union shapes itself in time. We see the fascinating dynamics – with countless variations and patterns – of the Covid crisis in our own countries, among our European neighbours, in America, Brazil and China. In the European Union, an alliance of 27 democracies, the picture is no different: leadership is perforce improvised, priorities collide, the alarmed public makes itself heard. Amid all the suffering and discord, this crisis has brought Europeans an intensified experience of joint political striving, a deepened awareness of a European *res publica*.

So the coronavirus works not only to expose hidden tendencies but to drive those tendencies, and with them the transition to a new European politics. As the latest crisis in a series, it pushes Europe further along the path towards a community of destiny that addresses events as a unified whole. In the high-stakes games surrounding the euro and the external borders, drama and conflict sought the public stage, independently of established frames of thought. Likewise, it is in the public sphere that the pandemic will spur the transformation of European politics, put it on stage and give it a new imperative. We have arrived at a fresh chapter in the passage to Europe.

Body politic

The Covid crisis, the latest in a series of ordeals, presents the European Union with specific difficulties. Never before did danger take the form of a direct, physical threat to the bodies of all citizens, without distinction – very different from the risks presented by rising interest rates or falling share values; different too from the undeniably dramatic but distant skirmishes on the external borders.

No wonder the consternation generated by this crisis has spread so far and so wide. Along with the underestimated resilience of the Union, along with the political deployment of controlled panic as an instrument of government, there was of course simply this: a highly uncertain and catastrophic situation, a matter of life and death, to which at the start no one had any answers.

The European Union certainly did not. It was forced to let go of its economic call for individual liberation and opt instead for physical protection. It had to turn its spatial self-image on its head. The watchword was no longer the removal of borders and barriers in order to allow freedom of movement across the whole continent; salvation would now come from erecting barriers and maintaining distance for the sake of its citizens' health. In this crisis too, a capacity to act based on expertise was invited onto unknown territory, equipped purely with improvisation.

Nobody disputes the unique medical and economic circumstances of the pandemic. Is disappointment or even bitterness regarding the European approach nevertheless justified?

A number of exculpatory marginal notes should be placed beside Europe's inadequate response to the wave of infection.

First, practically all governments reacted slowly and with disbelief to the initial outbreak of Covid-19. Compared to the vigilant South Korea, Taiwan or Japan, which had previous experience of such epidemics, the EU institutions in Brussels and the national governments in Rome, Paris, The Hague or Stockholm do not look good. But in 2020 there were places in the world – the United States, Brazil – where action was on some occasions more inadequate still.

Second, in all states with a federal territorial structure, tensions arose between the centre and the regions. In the US the White House tussled with the governors of the states. In the Federal Republic the *Länder* made their own appraisals of lockdown and face masks. In the UK, all four nations chose their own reopening schedules. In that light it is no surprise that the European Union, a political body with a weak centre, faced differences in approach between the member states.

Third, a marginal note highlighted by Brussels circles: public health is not an EU competence. This is true in a formal sense, but the point made no impression at all on the public. According to the treaty, the member states are responsible for the health of their citizens; the Union limits itself to the support, coordination and supplementation of national provision.[9] With regard to public health, therefore, the Brussels institutions are not in the first line of fire, as they were in the euro and refugee crises. The single currency and open internal borders are among the greatest accomplishments, both practical and symbolic, of a Union that has the powers required to sustain them. By contrast, problems in hospitals cannot strictly speaking be laid at the door of the EU. So why did that happen?

Perhaps recent experiences had a part to play. In previous crises the Union always took the leading role, and this was clearly another crisis, although a far more visceral one, since the threat was to the bodies of all citizens and it came from all sides. The global lockdown that made individual self-reliance ineffectual, the geo-medical divide-and-rule politics of China and America with their vaccine competition, a looming economic depression – all this made clear in an instant that "Europe" would have to do something. Whichever institution could and should lead the charge, it would at the very least need to have the political power of Europe as a whole at its disposal.

Ignorance, along with different historical perceptions and expectations of "Europe", quite commonly means that a fundamentally favourable attitude towards the EU can easily turn into unfounded disappointment or unjustified criticism. Take a complaint by Polish writer Olga Tokarczuk in late March 2020 in the *Frankfurter Allgemeine Zeitung*: "The European Union has forfeited the contest by leaving decision-making in this time of crisis to the nation states".[10] Definitely a missed penalty there, since the Nobel Prize winner ought to have known that in the Union no decision or law is made without input from the member states. As if it were a discovery, seasoned British journalist Simon Jenkins claimed in *The Guardian* that "the corona-crisis has exposed the truth about the EU: it's not a real union". From the examples he gives, it is evident that by "real union" he means a federal state like the US or a kingdom like the UK – a rather different thing.[11] The judgement of *Spiegel* columnist Nils Minkmar was pitiless: "The Europe that this Commission represents might as well be put out with the trash. It crumbled into a heap of rust as soon as people grabbed hold of it".[12] Unease, doom-mongering and distrust are weapons in the hands of lazy generalists.

Clear-headed criticism begins with a distinction between the Brussels world of treaties and institutions and the Union as a club of member states, or – and here I draw upon the toolkit of my earlier book *The Passage to Europe* – between the institutional "innermost sphere" and an "intermediate sphere" that encompasses national political institutions as well.[13] Interplay between the two spheres determines how Europe absorbs a dramatic event, and therefore also where it goes wrong. If "Europe" is to blame for the shortage of surgical masks in Italy, then whose fault is it exactly? The Commission, which neglected to build up stocks? Or other member states, such as Germany or France, which should have been quicker to offer help? An essential difference. Or ought the Commission to have forced the member states to come to Italy's aid? This latter reproach again presumes different institutional relationships, and therefore a different Treaty, placing the blame not with one or other of the players but with the constitutional shape of the Union: Europe is not what it ought to have been.

This goes to the heart of the matter. In the Covid crisis a gap was abruptly revealed between existing rules and the responsibility the situation called for. At such a moment it is for creative politics to construct bridges and institute reforms. An event such as this forces the Union to assume a shape it does not yet have. From the public we hear loud and clear, "This catastrophe is a public matter, affecting every European". The swelling cry of distress drowns out the usual dissenters who blow the whistle on every Brussels initiative as unwelcome interference in national affairs. As a call to arms, the cry also predates the assignation of competences in a treaty. So an appeal to the legal status quo ("not a competence") cannot provide a convincing defence against the reproach of inactivity.

In such circumstances the pandemic increases awareness, more than earlier European crises did, of a *res publica*. The public discovers that, sure, we share a currency and an external border, but it is our lives and our health that really matter to us. We watch intently all changes to the coronavirus situation in our own and neighbouring countries: the mortality figures, the lockdown rules, the face-mask and vaccination policy. We see very clearly the repercussions for our own lives of measures taken in other countries: the likelihood of infection, travel options, economic prospects. Thus a fierce Union-wide debate erupts about the appropriate joint response. A battle over the correct words and actions emerges from a fundamental engagement with the shared experience of the pandemic.

In the shaping of public affairs lies the task to be accomplished by political action. There too – as we shall see – lie the criteria by which to measure the Union's performance. So it is in a pandemic that threatens all its citizens that the Union is experiencing itself more than ever as a body politic, and a new public life is taking shape.

2

Metamorphosis: a different history of the Union

Every true history is contemporary history.

Benedetto Croce,
Theory and History of Historiography

Rules-politics and events-politics

The feeling that the slightest hiccough can take the European Union to the edge of the abyss is attributable to the metamorphosis it has undergone over recent decades, from a structure devoted purely to "rules-politics" to a set-up also capable of engaging in "events-politics". But insight into this gradual transformation is lacking. We will not understand the new Europe as long as we continue to look through the lens of the old.

That a revolution is happening before our eyes is the central tenet of this book. Over the past 30 years the operating procedure of the Union has changed fundamentally, with regard not just to who takes the decisions, and how and where they are taken, but to the way the Union is perceived, the way people observe European politics and why now more than ever they are demanding a direct say in a shared political life. It is a process of slow trends, shifting power relations and altered mentalities. All these changes have been accelerated, and sometimes exposed, by the acute shock of the pandemic. The urgency of the Covid crisis makes an interim analysis indispensable. What is happening? What has changed?

The institutions of the Union were originally designed principally to create a market and keep it in balance. This rules-politics is an ingenious mechanism that produces consensus and support, but it works only within the agreed system, and furthermore by dint of the fiction that history proceeds along predictable lines. In events-politics the aim is to get a grip on unforeseen, unanticipated situations. This form of political action is played out not within an established framework but precisely at moments when the framework itself is put to the test, in the most extreme cases by a war or catastrophe. In 2008 it was the credit crisis, when the economy refused any longer to adhere to the models relied upon by government bureaucracies. The response to an unforeseen situation can sometimes be to create a new regulatory framework, in which case we witness an interaction between events-politics and rules-politics, in a fairly common sequence. However, an acute political crisis demands that exceptional decisions are taken (not something that rules-politics is geared to).

Rules-politics requires politicians with the temperament and knowledge needed to engage in a balancing act. The public appreciates integrity and reliability, so in our democracies we often fail to perceive the difference between a politician and a civil servant or expert. Events-politics, by contrast, is all about leaders who are able to improvise. It is essential for them to find support in parliament and among the public with a convincing story as to why this or that decision is needed right now. Authority belongs to the ruler with the power to persuade, the ability to show courage and to determine the right moment to act.

For postwar Europe the choice was clear: rules-politics at the service of reconstruction and stability. Six expectant states deployed it from 1950 onwards. Events-politics was irrelevant. Should disturbances of the peace arise, Western Europe could seek refuge under the American umbrella. Brussels' ways of working and thinking were aimed at smothering political passions in a web of rules: depoliticization. Political conflicts with all their dramatic potential were transformed into manageable "problems" that were technically soluble. In the rule-making factory, conflicting interests and incompatible visions can be dealt with through a wondrous process of consultation and consideration, exchange and compromise, out of which the system then manufactures binding rules and norms for everyone, an internal market with policy coordination that spans practically an entire continent.

Yet the qualities of rules-politics can turn negative. A multiplicity of internal equilibriums can topple over into stagnation and indecision, while procedural caution can lead to bureaucratic sogginess and a loss of connection with the public. A third weakness is more immediately obvious: the rule-making factory is not set up to deal with sudden and widespread adversity, or the wholesale overstepping of boundaries or frameworks. Such moments of crisis therefore prise open the chest of rules. Gradually a new European politics has emerged as a result, which I call events-politics. A metamorphosis, whether we like it or not.

The factor of time brings the difference between events-politics and rules-politics most sharply into view. What to do if a eurozone country is on the verge of bankruptcy and to calm the markets the immense sum of €750 billion has to be put on the table within 72 hours, by means of endless phone calls and emergency talks? What if hundreds of thousands of refugees cross the Mediterranean in orange lifejackets, tens of thousands start marching across the Balkans and governments lose control of their borders? Or what if from one day to the next, because of a virus outbreak, businesses are threatened with ruin and millions of people will lose their jobs if the public coffers are not opened for them without delay?

In such cases of emergency the acute need for readiness trumps the bureaucratic preference for patience and caution. These are occasions not for endless regulation but for immediate decision-making and action. There is no time for attuning and ironing out, for months of consultation with white papers and green papers, for postponement until after an election or for patiently waiting until the problem blows over of its own accord. Instead there is a need for improvisation, for steering a course between law and historical necessity, because to wait or do nothing would be irresponsible. Ever since Europe grew to become more than a market, about which rules could be patiently negotiated, and as a Union involved a currency, a border and international politics, such situations of crisis and time pressure have presented themselves. There is no way back.

The major crises since 2008 have concerned not goat's cheese, lawn mowers or grain prices – the agenda of the Common Market – but billions of euros and solidarity, war and peace, identity and sovereignty, life and death. These are sensitive, passion-rousing matters of great importance to the public, and they cannot be depoliticized by means of technocratic or procedural ingenuity. The commotion arising from the crisis years represented a huge change from the quiet tedium of the heyday of rules-politics. True, the public liked to make fun of the bureaucratic craving for cucumber regulations, or to get wound up about red tape or incomprehensible prohibitions, and from time to time interest groups in one policy field or another (farmers, fishers) caused ructions on the roads to Brussels. Yet a large majority of voters accepted the Europe of the market with a shrug, as long as the system created jobs and increased prosperity. Political scientists called this compliant indifference "permissive consensus".

But when danger threatens, tensions rise, bringing onto the scene, after the ticking clock, a second striking contrast between rules-politics and events-politics: the involvement of the public.

How differently people experienced these continental crises. Gone were the afflictions of dullness and tedium. During the euro crisis and the refugee crisis, all the television news broadcasts and all the major newspapers opened day after day with the latest twists and turns in a Union-wide storyline. Before the eyes of the world, squares from Athens to Madrid and Rome filled with defiant demonstrators. Voters discovered the ballot box as a means of settling scores with national leaders for their visible, European performances. Previously marginal parties of protest made serious bids for power based on dissatisfaction with currency politics or immigration affairs. The British choice between remaining and leaving held the country and its neighbours in suspense for years: in or out; stick or twist? And in the middle of the pandemic opinion-makers on all sides watched a diplomatic dance over hundreds of billions of euros for recovery funds – once again a crucial moment of truth. With and within events, all citizens of the Union were addressed, and Europe was at stake in a visible battle: a public matter.

The demands of time and the public bring us to the third major difference between rules- and events-politics, the players. Rapid and controversial decisions in times of crisis call for political authority, for visible and decisive powers of persuasion. When a storm gets up, the bureaucratic and technocratic authority available in Brussels falls short, including that of commissioners, parliamentarians and sectoral ministers who work in the same style, and of the people who keep the daily rules-machinery running. In events-politics other political players step onto the stage in the form of 27 elected presidents and premiers. In the euro crisis it was the heads of state or government, gathered together under the leadership of the German chancellor and the French president, who from 2010 onwards defended a multiplicity of emergency decisions before the national tribunes and thereby – along with the central bankers in Frankfurt – saved the besieged currency. This was a radical turn away from the old rules-politics, in which national leaders were deliberately kept outside the door. With new executive organs, adjusted voting rules and permanent presidencies, the Union is establishing itself in a world that demands agility and vigour, and accountability. So Europe's metamorphosis, spurred on by time and the public, takes effect on the terrain of institutional form and personal embodiment.

There is a legitimate question as to whether events-politics is not, in disguise, the politics of a permanent state of emergency. This is an obvious risk, not least in the Covid crisis, which in contrast to earlier crises threatens all citizens physically.

In reaching a judgement it is best to avoid extremes. On one side stands the lawyer who, with Martin Luther,[1] proposes "*Fiat iustitia, et pereat mundus*", "Let justice be done, though the world perish".* On the other side stands the politician, who tackles the pandemic crisis with a motto of their own, "Necessity knows no law".

It is rarely as black and white as that. Embedded rules-politics exists on the same greyscale as the events-politics that parries surprises.[2] Both are needed. By means of regulations, politics creates an environment with a high degree of certainty, indispensable in all societies. But an unexpected situation does not conform to existing rules. There always remains a crack through which uncontrolled events, unintended consequences or new desires can squeeze, requiring decision, action and persuasion. What is played out then is the transition from "governance" to "government", from anonymous, multi-layered administration to the plainly visible authority of a government, from bureaucratic or legal competences to political responsibility.

After the war: promise and taboo

Three historical moments were decisive for the passage from a Brussels rule-making factory to a European community of destiny: the foundation after 1945, the refoundation after

---

* In the euro crisis this belief seemed to be held by some members of the German Constitutional Court, in a variation on "*Fiat pactum, et pereat moneta*": not a cent to the South, though the euro perish.

1989 and the crises from 2008 onwards.[3] These were three historical situations in which the European states were forced to reconsider their position in time – in defiance of existing habits and patterns of thought that threatened to stifle a new self-understanding.

The work of German historian Reinhart Koselleck can help us to understand how history operates. He has coined the term "sediments of time". Like their geological model, these are "several layers of time of differing duration and differentiable origin, which are nonetheless present and effectual at the same time". He believes that all conflicts, compromises and agreements can theoretically be traced back to tensions and fault lines between different temporal layers.[4]

For political Europe, the founding years were one such fundamental layer of time, and in language and mentality it continues to make itself felt. This is most clearly visible in the principle of legal and political depoliticization, an approach that enabled the founders to guide any excess of political passion, which had been fatal for Europe before 1945, into safer channels. Bureaucratic tenacity, tardiness and tedium as a remedy for war: a brilliant idea. The strategy of undermining drama and conflict and keeping it out of the picture proved effective.[5] But this approach came at the price of a steady erosion of public and political powers of persuasion. The right to speak about Europe fell to economists, lawyers and EU ideologues, who addressed themselves not to citizens but to stakeholders. With their jargon, acronyms and self-congratulation they drove even the most interested members of the public to distraction. Which was awkward, because the metamorphosis of rules-politics into events-politics demands not just practical adroitness but open communication with the assembled public. A story, a battle of words, an exchange of ideas, responsibility – in our day the voter wants to hear, see and speak.

Less noticed but at least as essential is the time perspective given to Europe by its founders. They proclaimed a new era, with an end to war: Europe as a promise. The key to this auspicious future was Jean Monnet's axiom that the interweaving of economic interests makes war materially impossible, along with the institutional prescription that goes with it, the "Community method". The Brussels depoliticization machine therefore had another task besides the production of rules: to influence discourse and to proselytize, which meant that the rhetorical power of the promise must be used to the full.

The promise of a new era has an important corollary: a permanent claim on the future. The Brussels world of offices lives, as it were, "on credit". That is the only way to maintain the connection between a modest beginning and an ambitious end goal. People like to talk of "the European project", a future-oriented undertaking. The founders equipped their Promise with two visions. One was of geographical expansion, with more states taking part, perhaps one day the entire continent. The other was communitarization, providing mining, agriculture and trade policy with new rules and then extending them into neighbouring policy areas. This permanent claim on the future produced the Brussels tendency to translate every "not" as a "not yet". Certain powers had "not yet" been transferred, the Parliament had "not yet" gained the support of the voters, Poland is "not yet" a member of the eurozone – nothing is what it is; only becoming counts. Moreover, movement is presumed to be in one direction, towards more competences, more members, "more Europe". Hence the bewilderment when in 2016 British voters broke the spell of the future and demanded a future all of their own. They had done something unthinkable.

This inherent impulsion is consistent with a Treaty venerated as a sheet anchor. The founding document contains from the very start an invitation to its own revision. Its originality in this respect means that institutional or substantive reform, in international law generally regarded as a violation of the established order, can be conceived as confirmation of its spirit. Anyone refusing change needs to provide justification. In that sense, from 1973 onwards the British discovered that they had joined not just a market but a club with continually changing rules and functions, an "ever closer union". In those three famous words – driven by a legal practice of teleological interpretation and justified by future-oriented aims in the preamble and the opening clauses – the European impulsion finds its expression. The intimate connection between movement and order, between project and treaty, determines the mentality of the Brussels inner sphere, where life is lived between treaty and law.

In 1950, faith in a new future generated the courage and energy to build something unprecedented out of nothing, but over time it ossified into an orthodoxy that tolerated no aberration or alternative. In the uncompromising slogan of Paul-Henri Spaak, the project's Belgian pacesetter, "Europe will be supranational or it will be nothing".[6]

The dream of a new beginning necessitates the banishment of the evil past. Here we come up against the reverse side of the promise: the taboo. The break between past and present had to be total.

The greatest taboo of all was the appeal to national interest. To violate it was to place oneself outside the order. When in 1965 French president Charles de Gaulle recalled his ambassador from Brussels, one European commissioner called it the worst thing that had happened to Europe "since Hitler". Margaret Thatcher declared "we want our money back". Thirty years later, this statement – sharpened by myth-making into "my money back" – was still engraved on the collective memory, which in itself is enough to suggest that the British prime minister had contravened a prohibition. Which? It was not so much that she was counting her pennies. All diplomats from all the member states calculate how much they are receiving from the collective pot. But you must not admit it out loud. The affront lay in Thatcher's tone and her insistence that it was "our" (British) money. Little remained of the notion that it was shared European money. She had ostentatiously demonstrated that she did not believe in the promise. Even now, many years after De Gaulle and Thatcher, interference by national leaders in EU affairs in Brussels is regarded with suspicion. Some see it as regression, as the "renationalization of European politics" – rather than a developing "Europeanization of national politics".[7]

A second taboo prohibits speaking in terms of differences between member states. The Community is a community of equals. Disparity in power is the main unmentionable difference. Everyone knows that France has more power at the negotiating table than Luxembourg, but you must not say so. In the juridical sphere all are equal. This fiction of equality before the law is effective and useful, and the smaller member states in particular are attached to it. Even though power imbalances do not in practice disappear, the law tempers them. The problem is that other differences are imagined away as well. All member states are expected to be the same, or at least to become the same, as suggested by the promising vocabulary of "harmonization", "convergence" and "integration". Although for their embedding in rules-politics this is perhaps a necessary presumption, with action in events-politics it is a different story. It does matter what you are able or willing to do as a member state, what your geographical position is, or your historical experience, whether or not you have an army, or are capable of raising taxes or guarding your borders. Although these self-evident truths came to light in recent crises, it remains tricky to say that some member states are different.

A third taboo is against asking about the location of the Union's government. The Community, the lawyers said, is *sui generis*, a thing apart. Its institutions and functions cannot be arranged according to the classic constitutional categories of Montesquieu's separation of powers. Even when the Community was given a Parliament, it was regarded as naive to ask where the Government was to be found. Years later, this taboo led to a revealing semantic battle. Every time Paris declared that the euro needed an "economic government", Berlin and The Hague responded that they preferred "economic governance", not visible decision-makers but rules and procedures.

A fourth and final taboo concerns talking about a border. This prohibition is understandable given the promise of a radical break with the past. The new Europe must be open and inviting, border-free. Borders are reminiscent of border disputes, war, the will to power – the evil past. This taboo too is persistent. Despite enlargement with new members, despite the disappearance of internal borders, the issue remains fraught. What is the external border? Where does political Europe stop? The taboo is challenged, and not just by neighbouring countries Ukraine, Russia and Turkey. The European public too wants an answer.

There is a logic to the taboo strategy. Initially the Community was a delicate greenhouse seedling that needed to be protected against forces within national governments, bureaucracies or legal systems. The moral delegitimization of opposition was effective. Seventy years on, this *raison d'être* has fallen away and the strategy has become a handicap. In a whirl of events the Union needs to defend our interests and put them into words, while the member states, through their own efforts, need to combine their capacities to act, jointly determining a position in space and time. Nevertheless, the postwar dream of a new era without power persists. This became particularly clear after 1989.

After the Wall: breakthrough and resistance

For Europe's event-driven metamorphosis, the fall of the Berlin Wall was the "mother shock", the historical big bang that forced the European states into a fundamental re-evaluation. Just as the Paris speech by a French minister on 9 May 1950 gave the initial impulse for the founding of the Community (1951), so the Berlin shock of 9 November 1989 resulted in the founding of the Union (1992). A New Beginning. It led to fascinating skirmishes between the Promise and the historical reality, to a confusing period in which old and new forms, Community and Union, existed alongside each other and mixed together.

After the popular uprisings of 1989 in Central and Eastern Europe – in the autumn in Berlin and Leipzig, in the spring

in Warsaw, and at various times in Prague, Bucharest, Budapest and Sofia – the need for Europe as a whole to engage in
events-politics was generally recognized for the first time.
Within two years, in Maastricht, the 12 government leaders
endorsed this realization in a Union Treaty. A breakthrough.
The shock of 1989 had been too great; the Union burst out of
its rules-politics corset. The metamorphosis became visible.

Three new paths were traced out. First, the Union would
concern itself with security. During the Cold War that responsibility had largely been left to the US, but new uncertainties
about borders and geostrategic power relations had emerged.
What was in prospect for the eastern half of the continent
following the withdrawal of the Russians? Economic chaos?
Civil war? And after the withdrawal of the United States
from the western half? What position would a united Germany demand in the new Europe? At the insistence of France,
the Union Treaty signed in Maastricht contained clauses
about a common foreign and security policy. Even the idea
of a future common defence policy was included, despite
British resistance. Wary of the power vacuum on the eastern border, members of the Union decided in 1993 to offer
their ex-communist neighbouring states the prospect of
membership. Of course the expansion of the market by some
100 million consumers was of considerable importance, but
the eastward enlargement, which became a reality from 2004
onwards, was motivated primarily by security considerations.[8]
The new Germany especially, no longer split between East
and West, pressed for it. Territorial expansion as security
policy.

The second new path involved the introduction of a common currency. That too was decided at Maastricht. The

technical plans were ready, but the radical elimination of currencies, most of them centuries old, was decided upon only as a result of the shock of the fall of the Berlin Wall. The French president, concerned about shifting power relations, made his country's agreement on a common currency a test of Germany's attachment to the European club. The German chancellor understood that reasoning. Typifying the post-Wall tensions, this intrinsic renewal took shape according to the model of rules-politics, with the euro as an extension of the market. After Paris forced from it the major concession that there would be a common currency, Bonn was allowed to determine what it would look like. To guarantee price stability comparable to that provided by the Deutschmark, and to prevent reciprocal financial liability, it wanted to keep the currency at a safe distance from political caprice. Hence the outsourcing of monetary policy to an independent central bank; hence the embedding of budgetary policy in strict rules; hence too the ban on financing each other's debts.

This German and Dutch preference for a depoliticized currency fitted wonderfully well with Brussels thinking. For the experts, monetary union was not an unprecedented historical and political leap but a logical next step in the successful integration of the internal market, which had for some years included the free movement of capital. Countries with other ideas, such as France, resigned themselves for the time being to this vision. The UK, by contrast, refused to commit itself to the single currency. For London it was a step that went far beyond the boundaries of rules-politics, so Britain kept the pound. Thus with Maastricht the game of exceptions began, of opt-outs and opt-ins. In this recognition of differences, something else announced itself too: the fall of the Promise.

The third path of renewal in the Union lay through the politicization of the institutions, with stronger links with citizens and voters. Europe's institutional structure is the outcome of decades of teamwork and rivalry, between France and Germany, between large and small countries, between national capitals and the central institutions. There has never been agreement on an optimal structure. If we look at political life as a theatre – with players and public, stage and wings, a performance in time and space – then we see that from the start three dramaturgical styles have been deployed: depoliticization, parliamentarization and summitry. Whereas before 1989 the first of these dominated, afterwards the other two gained the upper hand. To get a clear impression of the substance of the sediments of time, identification of this trio of styles and traditions is needed.

First there is the depoliticizing Community, within which three institutions organize affairs. The Commission in Brussels makes proposals, carries out specific tasks and acts as "guardian of the treaties". From Luxembourg the Court of Justice watches over the Treaty and defends the emerging legal order. The Council of Ministers provides a forum in which ministers of the national governments negotiate and determine the rules that will then do the depoliticizing work. Functionaries in all the institutions have always known that reaching compromises and interweaving interests happens most smoothly out of sight of the public. In theatrical terms, they share a preference for working behind the scenes. Public support is derived not from democratic participation but from practical results.

From the 1960s onwards, two dramaturgical interventions were used in an effort to put the public and the citizen on stage in this depoliticized setting, over time resulting in a European Parliament and a European Council of heads of state and government. Both aspire to enable a common political life to tread the boards. There was disagreement about how to involve the public and in what capacity, and about who should take the central role. One intervention, favoured in (West-)Germany, Italy, Belgium and Luxembourg, and drawing energy from the Promise, aimed to create a direct link between Parliament and voters in their European capacity in order to furnish the Commission with legitimacy as a kind of government. The other intervention, driven by France, was an attempt to present on the stage, to a multifarious public of national voters, the government leaders as the central figures, so that events-politics could be engaged in too. For a long time the two approaches distrusted and obstructed each other, until in 1974 French president Giscard d'Estaing brought about an agreement that established both the European Council and direct elections to the European Parliament (every five years from 1979 onwards). The member states built upon this compromise in Maastricht in 1991. At the request of the Germans, the Parliament, which up to then had provided only very limited consultative rights, was given legislative power alongside the Council of Ministers, while the European Council, although in practice this periodic summit of government leaders had already grown to become the highest decision-making power, was invested with formal responsibilities for the first time, at the instigation of the French, especially in the fields of foreign and judicial policy. With these decisions the leaders recognized that a Union that engages in events-politics needs the support and the voices of voters. The question of who had the highest authority remained unanswered: time would tell. This was politicization without government.

The public is well aware that Europe changed shape after 1989. During the process of ratification by the 12 national parliaments and populations, the Maastricht Treaty encountered unprecedented resistance. In June 1992 Danish voters rejected the Union in a referendum because of its political innovations (such as the currency). That rejection was a novelty and a shock. Then French voters, after a divisive debate, said "yes" but only by an extremely narrow margin. In the UK the prime minister pulled a recalcitrant House of Commons into line by means of a dramatic vote of confidence. In the Federal Republic the judges in Karlsruhe, with their stern "thus far and no further" Maastricht-Urteil (1993) set themselves up as the voice of German voters. A perplexed Brussels experienced the critical responses of national electorates, parliaments and high courts as sledgehammer blows. The tumult over Europe incontrovertibly began with this passage to the Union. The public had stood up and was out of its seats, a liberating sensation.

Astonishingly, forces were at work during this period that attempted to obscure the metamorphosis and smother the public outcry. The tectonic shift was opposed with all the might of Brussels practice and doctrine. The Commission and Parliament regarded the institutional arrangements of the Maastricht Treaty as infringements of the sacred Community method, as incompatible with the pure doctrine. On the festive occasion at which the Union treaty was signed, Jacques Delors was in his own words "a disappointed man".[9] The key role for government leaders, the separate procedure for foreign policy and for justice and home affairs: these must – still today

– be no more than temporary exceptions. As ever, "not" was translated as "not yet".

After the Wall the quarrel grew fiercer. The Union is a political pact, which, in order to tame events, broke with depoliticization. This heightened the battle between the two political interventions: politicization via either the Parliament or summits of national leaders. On the authority of the founding promise, advocates of the parliamentary model liked to see the power struggle as a moral conflict between the Community (good) and the Union (bad). They refused to take into account the demands made by events-politics, the requirement of governmental authority that arises when crisis decisions must be made. This was ideological vilification as the obverse of technocratic arrogance. The advocates of summits found in the crises their historical justification, but they underestimated the extent to which improvisation or the will to power of a small number of leaders scuppers the intricate mesh of rules-politics and disrupts mutual trust.

Angela Merkel experienced the doctrinaire reaction at first hand. In a speech in Bruges in 2010 she pointed out that the Commission and Parliament do not have a monopoly on "Europe", and that through the Council of Ministers and the European Council (of which she was a member) the member states also play a role in the Union. To describe the intended interplay between institutions and member states, the chancellor floated, with insights borne out of sediments of time, the term "Union method".[10] It fitted the situation perfectly, but touched a nerve in Brussels circles. There were cries of shame; its deployment was taken to be an attack.[11] Merkel had violated a taboo. Under pressure from prominent party colleagues in the European Parliament, she dropped the term. Although the Community has since been formally dissolved,[12] the "Community method" remains inviolable. Thus the old thinking restricts Europe's understanding of itself. The unyielding faith that the "true Europe" must be built in defiance of the member states, rather than with them, feeds public scepticism and stands in the way of the development of a joint capacity to act.

It was not doctrinaire counter-pressure alone that impeded understanding of the European *Wende*. Already in 1989 the idea took root that the mission of a new Union – to guarantee security and engage in events-politics – was less than urgent. The shockwave of the fall of the Wall, the return of major issues of peace and war, seemed to ebb quickly away. The return of history had certainly set diplomatic cogs in motion, and indeed brought about the breakthrough to the Union, but it had barely any effect on Europe's self-image. In fact in a final outburst of neocolonial optimism, the West embraced the idea of the End of History, the tempting notion that the entire world was on its way to the free and democratic capitalism of the Western model. What irony. At the very moment when Europe made its entrance on the geopolitical stage, an American declared, "The performance is over. You can go back to the dressing rooms".

But Francis Fukuyama, the prophet of the end of history, had failed to notice tremors and tectonic shifts in the earth beneath. Acceleration continued and the return of history became visible, first in 2001 and very clearly from 2008 onwards. Since then, Europe's metamorphosis has taken place in front of our eyes in a series of crises, and a dauntless public is vying for a role in determining history's course.

In the crises: the experience of vulnerability

In his brilliant study *The Machiavellian Moment* (1975), J. G. A.
Pocock locates the creation of modern political thought – by
Machiavelli and contemporaries such as Guicciardini – in the
recognition of the finite nature of the polis. Pocock speaks of
the moment "in which the republic was seen as confronting its
own temporal finitude, as attempting to remain morally and
politically stable in a stream of irrational events conceived
as essentially destructive of all systems of secular stability".[13]
Those who know themselves to be mortal must regard and
arm themselves as chance entities in the river of time: an existential experience.

The European Union has found itself in such a moment of
historical-political awakening for more than ten years now.
A Machiavellian moment, in Pocock's sense. The summer
of 2008 served as a tipping point, because of the volatile war
between Russia and Georgia in the Caucasus and the relentless implosion of merchant bank Lehman Brothers in New
York just a few weeks later. In August a war in the East, in September a meltdown in the West: history had shifted up a gear.

A concatenation of events followed: invasion and revolt,
financial crisis and depression, migration and deterrence, the
rise and fall of great powers, a pandemic with death walking
abroad – phenomena from an almost forgotten past, cele-
brating their comeback in a whirling present. Disbelieving,
unaccustomed and improvising, the European states and their
peoples, alone and together, stood firm.

Through major crises between 2008 and 2021, the Union
found itself forced to let go of the sacred framework of its per-
petuity thinking and act in the immediate here and now, to

resist and survive the disasters that threatened. The new and unexpected requirement made of them was to be geared for contingency and engage in events-politics.

The financial tidal wave of September 2008 gave American and European politicians, policy-makers and central bankers the shock of their lives. With robust interventions by the states they warded off the danger. A year and a half later a "second Lehman" threatened, for Europe alone. An approaching Greek bankruptcy jeopardized the currency. The Union improvised a way out. Of necessity, leaders in the euro crisis (2010–12) made short work of monetary depoliticization. They decided on central banking supervision, a massive rescue fund and regular summits, and quietly assented to the purchase of government bonds by the Central Bank – steps unthinkable shortly before. The survival of the currency required stricter rules, but also a combined political will, a monetary capacity to act and an ability to persuade the public when faced with markets and voters.

Next to put Europe's self-image to the test were dramas on the borders. The geopolitical crises surrounding Ukraine (2014–15) and migration (2015–16) presented the Union, which had always preferred to speak about universal values than about its own interests, with tragic choices: between justice and peace, between security and hospitality. It inevitably lost its innocence. To staunch the torrent of refugees from Syria, government leaders made an ethically and legally dubious deal with President Erdoğan's Turkey. To bring the war between Ukraine and Russia – the most dangerous outburst of violence on the continent since the Balkan Wars – under control, Chancellor Merkel and President Hollande arranged a compromise between the Ukrainian president and his Russian counterpart. In emergencies the Union must close borders, disavow principles, get its hands dirty. It prefers not to say so in as many words, but action it is.

Only after the double whammy of Brexit and Trump, meted out in 2016, did the words come. "It is time for us as Europeans to take our destiny into our own hands", said Angela Merkel in May 2017, just a few days after the American president pulled the rug out from under Europe's security guarantees. A distinctly Machiavellian statement. Her German-European consciousness could be sure of support from the French-European Emmanuel Macron, newly installed as president in Paris, who was eager to make his presence felt on the world stage on the Union's behalf. The chancellor also derived confidence from the united front shown by Europe after the British referendum of June 2016. The divorce made everyone tremble; for a moment the Union feared for its survival, but the 27 regrouped and lined up in battle array against the leaver. Out of the experience of its own vulnerability, a new will to live came to the fore.

It is striking that during the double ordeal of Brexit-&-Trump, the European Union operated more convincingly and harmoniously than in the crises that preceded it. Why did this of all moments generate a strength of will that seemed lacking before? Previous abysses were no less deep: the euro turbulences, the America vs Russia war by proxy in eastern Ukraine, the freezing refugees in the Macedonian snow. So why was this the moment to "take our destiny into our own hands"?

The short answer is: Germany. The dual electoral assault on the international order of 2016 shook the Federal Republic awake, making manifest the country's geopolitical vulnerability. The contrast with earlier crisis management was stark.

43

In the euro crisis Berlin had experienced itself as the strong triple-A economy called upon to save weaker siblings. In the Ukraine crisis, far from home, federal chancellor Angela Merkel was the continental chief diplomat and peacemaker. In the refugee crisis the country stood alone with its open border policy, in the role of a Good Samaritan. Challenges, certainly, but Germany did not see its positive self-image marred, indeed it was reinforced. The shocks reverberating from the Brexit vote and the Trump election, however, impacting on the postwar economic and geopolitical order, were unprecedented.

The experience of vulnerability, at a moment of relative strength, gave the political leadership in Berlin the self-confidence to say "take our destiny into our own hands". But why "we Europeans" and not "we Germans"? Because the European alliance is of vital importance for Germany; only by reference to "Europe" can a German government argue that geopolitics is necessary and unavoidable. Whereas throughout the Cold War (when the Soviet Union had East Germany in its grip) West Germany needed America for its security and France for the redemption-from-sin framework of "Europe", both those aspects now coincided conceptually for the first time. So Germany invested its political energy in the Union and Merkel took the lead in organizing a united European front. In Macron she discovered the first postwar French president to recognize that Europe had become too big merely to serve as leverage for French power and projects, and that as a Union it must be able to put a political will and power of its own on stage.

For France and the other member states it is important to realize that this new German political strength of will manifests itself in a striving for European sovereignty, rather than

German nationalism. A great blessing, historically speaking. Meanwhile, Germany will have to temper its rules-politics instincts and lay aside its faith in the Brussels salvation story in which every new crisis carries within it the Promise of a united Europe.*

Merkel's historic words of 2017 were followed by two or three years of languid political reorientation in Berlin. No action. This somewhat self-satisfied hesitation aroused resentment in the always impatient Paris. The fact is, the chancellor had got ahead of her domestic troops; the Atlantic traditions in the German foreign policy establishment are tenacious. Moreover, Poland and other Eastern European neighbours placed more trust in Washington even under Trump than in Brussels or Berlin. Hence it was only a fifth major crisis, the pandemic of 2020, that convinced the German public of its historical responsibilities and spurred the federal chancellor to act.

---

* One example immediately shows how Germany plays chess on several boards at once. On 24 June 2016, of all days, with the Union in shock at the result of the British referendum, president of the European Parliament Martin Schulz and German vice-chancellor Sigmar Gabriel, party colleagues, declared in a jointly written paper, "We must now work further to make the European Commission in the future into a real European government, a government that is controlled parliamentarily by the European Parliament and a second chamber of member states" (Sigmar Gabriel and Martin Schulz, "Europa neu gründen", *Spiegel Online*).

Entr'acte

From now on it can be said that plague was the concern of all of us. Hitherto, surprised as he may have been by the strange things happening around him, each individual citizen had gone about his business as usual, so far as this was possible... But once the town gates were shut, every one of us realized that all, the narrator included, were, so to speak, in the same boat, and each would have to adapt himself to the new conditions of life.

Albert Camus, *The Plague*[1]

A public affair

"Where is Europe when you need it?" was the question asked everywhere in the spring of 2020 as the virus sowed sickness and ruin in that part of the world. An initial cry for help in Italy and Spain, it reverberated across the Union and soon echoed back as a sneering gibe from Moscow and Beijing, and even from Brexit London. The situation was of course grave. On 11 March 2020, the WHO declared the Covid outbreak a worldwide pandemic and two days later it identified the European continent as its epicentre.[2] That professional assessment by the global health authorities shook a continental sense of safety. "Here? At home?" Meanwhile images of virologists in spacesuits, abandoned dead in hospital corridors and cavalcades of Covid coffins fed the fear for life and limb. Against this macabre backdrop it was striking that the European Union at first did nothing at all to ease the suffering, and the breathless defence that the Brussels institutions had no formal competence in the field of public health was experienced as feeble in the extreme.

The actions of the European states and their Union in the Covid crisis should be judged through the lens of events-politics. History was knocking at the door. On such occasions a lack of formal powers is no excuse (nor necessarily a reason for criticism). What counts is the capacity demonstrated in the situation at hand to engage jointly in events-politics, to identify and parry a shock affecting all citizens, to improvise, to convince straight away and, by extension, to anticipate events and strengthen the system. This benchmark is dynamic and relates specifically to the active deployment of political responsibilities.

Responsibility is a political notion, one that invites action. It plays out in a different domain from that of the competences familiar to EU lawyers and officials. Unprecedented crises demand by definition a degree of authority and a power to act that goes beyond customary capacities; in such situations an appeal is made to a leader's personal responsibility. When reality throws up a problem – a currency under pressure, migrants at the border, a virus ripping through the population – a response must follow. The etymology is relevant. In "responsibility" lies "response". Taking responsibility is the visible expression of a sense of duty (as becomes clear when it is not taken). Yet ultimately it is a voluntary act. No one can be forced to take responsibility. The invitation presumes a question for which no standard answer lies ready, a problem that has not been set down in rules or agreements, a cry for help with no obvious place to turn.*

The sequence of problem and response helps to illuminate the exceptional dynamic of the Covid crisis and reveals something essential about European politics. Let us turn for a moment to John Dewey and his still vital book *The Public and its Problems* (1927), about the nature of the state. While most political theories attribute the origin of the state to the actions and willpower of founders and go-getters, Dewey turns things around: the public came first. A public forms as a reaction to incidents that affect people in general. These may be events coming at them from outside, or it might be a matter of the indirect consequences of human activities. An agreement between two friends to go fishing remains private; an agreement between two conspirators or two monopolists will affect other people as well. As soon as such indirect consequences are experienced or observed, Dewey writes, a public exists. At first it is formless, divided and unorganized, but once attempts have been made to organize the public and, in its name, to resist, promote or react in some way to the effects of human actions or other events, "something having the traits of a state comes into existence".[3] To protect the interests of the public, official bearers of authority step forward (politicians, judges, officials). The Romans called the requisite buildings, possessions, funds and other resources *res publica*, a public matter.

---

* We therefore need to distinguish between this creative, political responsibility and responsibility as discipline, a term frequently used in Brussels that lies in the sphere of member countries conforming to self-imposed rules or doing their homework.

By extension the term stands for the entirety of public interests. Public affairs are both a task (the public good) and a form (commonwealth, republic).

The needs of the public change continually, as Dewey stresses, and nobody can predict how. After all, a public comes into existence as a reaction to largely unforeseen events and developments. Moreover, serving the public interest has consequences of its own. Mistakes, misjudgements, impractical laws and abuses of power are commonplace. Since the situation changes all the time, the demands of the public change too, which is what public debate is all about. The implication – and this aspect is somewhat underplayed by Dewey – is that the public may be divided in the way it acts or reacts. Not everyone will draw the same conclusions from a shared experience of events. Joint involvement in a public matter does not necessarily produce a single "will of the people".

States differ in time and place, as do ideas about what is or is not an affair of state. Yet Dewey sees certain constants. Inventions, discoveries and new ideas tend to be a matter of private initiative, whereas the state is more focused on that which is established and lasting. The public generally feels concern for a weaker party and demands protection for it. "Legislatures", Dewey writes in 1927, "are more ready to regulate the hours of labor of children than of adults, or women than of men".[4] The public call for action by the state is loudest when the direct consequences of an event or the indirect consequences of human acts are "of importance". This criterion is vague, the author admits, but not meaningless. Three factors give consequences greater importance: their far-reaching character in time or space, their settled, uniform and recurrent nature, and their irreparableness.

Lastly, Dewey has a sharp eye for the tension that can arise between a "new public", as the response to a new historical situation, and existing political institutions. "To form itself, the [new] public has to break existing political forms. This is hard to do because these forms are themselves the regular means of instituting change".[5] This new public exists alongside an "old" public, which is attached to existing connections, familiar answers, established frameworks. A new public can use periodic elections to make its wishes known, to get policy adjusted, to replace the players, but it is committed to the electoral framework as such. Adapting the form of the state soon requires a revolution.

More than in previous major European crises, we see how during the Covid catastrophe political action follows a public call for something to be done. By contrast, the financial storms of 2008 onwards were calmed top-down. Governments together, alarmed by central bankers and experts, had to convince reluctant parliaments of the need for drastic decisions to save the banking system and the currency. The public looked on, not having asked for anything. Similarly, the economic freedoms introduced by the Brussels rule-making factory from 1957 onwards were bestowed from on high, as a favour, not extracted from below as a demand, and the same goes for the new statute of political citizenship that in 1992 accompanied the transformation of the Community into the Union. There was no citizens' rights movement marching on Brussels, Luxembourg or the national capitals. As Dewey might say, there was of course a European public, but it was "inchoate, unorganized", barely had a voice and did not give forceful direction, except to apply the brakes or to say "no".[6] Political movement and action came uninvited.

A spur to the primacy of the public was the migrant crisis of 2015–16. Confronted with dramatic pictures of refugees landing on the Greek coast and moving northwards pushing carts, public opinion demanded action. The public was deeply divided, however. A call for compassion and open borders collided with a call for security and the closing of borders.

Clearer still is the primacy of the public amid the pandemonium of the pandemic. The public says, "Our lives and our health are a public matter. We want politicians to take responsibility, to help us, to protect the weak and prevent irreparable loss of life". At that point the *res publica* already exists as a task and assignment, but as yet without being translated into constitutional forms or legal instruments. The political response needs to be developed through improvisation, its tools designed on the spot. Unlike the experts of the status quo, the lawyers and bureaucrats, we demand of leading politicians that they face up to the dynamics of a situation. Giving shape to change in public is their calling and their profession.

I will examine this fascinating interplay between public and politics in three steps, beginning with a chronicle of the Covid crisis through the lens of events-politics (Chapter 3). Then I look at the part played by this unique episode in the metamorphosis that the Union is going through in the direction of visibility and openness (Chapter 4). Finally, we shall see that because of the pandemic, the public is beginning to regard Europe's geostrategic position in between acting or floundering great powers as "its business" (Chapter 5).

3

Chronicle of the coronavirus crisis

Certain it is, the greatest part of the poor or families who formerly lived by their labour, or by retail trade, lived now on charity; and had there not been prodigious sums of money given by charitable, well-minded Christians for the support of such, the city could never have subsisted.

Daniel Defoe, *A Journal of the Plague Year*

A threefold response

As an event the coronavirus crisis is reminiscent of those concentric ripples that form when a stone is tossed into a pond.[1] The first circle represents the immediate impact of the virus: fear, sickness, death. The next stands for the initial protective response, such as the closing of borders, while the third expanding circle is that of increasing unemployment and shrinking economies. The fourth and final circle represents geopolitics. How great powers manifest themselves on the world stage during such a crisis – which depends in part on how successfully they have tackled it at home – can determine essential global strategies for years if not decades to come.

A chronicle of the European response to the first three consequences of the pandemic – for public health, freedom of movement and economic activity – makes clear how, in essence, events-politics works. The fourth consequence, its geopolitical impact, deserves a separate analysis, which follows in Chapter 5. In the unprecedented dilemmas with which the Covid crisis confronts policy-makers, these three consequences can rarely be addressed separately, yet the lens of events-politics focuses best when they are each taken in turn; this is why the chronicle in this chapter proposes separate timelines, in part parallel (within each Act), in part sequential. To absorb and parry the shock to public health, the Union, poorly equipped, could at the start do little other than improvise a response. In recent crises it had gained experience in border politics and financial policy, so in those two areas we should in theory have been able to expect a more rapid and effective performance.

Each government is responsible for the health of its own citizens, according to the rules of the Union. What makes the Covid crisis politically intriguing is that the public was the first to regard tackling the pandemic as part of the European *res publica* – because of the speed of the virus in crossing borders, the disastrous prospect of locking down the economy and the immediate threat to everybody's health. My attention is therefore focused on the breakthroughs, big and small, in political recognition of the coronavirus disaster as a European public matter.

We shall see how a first, rather intense sequence of events played out between the initial virus outbreak and the summer of 2020, before a second sequence unfolded in winter and spring 2021. Tussles around face masks, closed borders and

rescue funds took centre stage in Act I, whereas further financial disputes and vaccine wars dominated Act II.

Act I

SICKNESS AND HEALTH
(24 JANUARY–31 JULY 2020)

Engaging in events-politics begins with the capacity to identify danger and face up to its impact.

On 24 January 2020 France reported Europe's first three
cases of the new virus, all of them traced back to visits to
China. This did not lead to either governmental dynamism or
political panic. The Stockholm-based EU agency for infectious
diseases declared the next day, "Even if there are still many
things unknown about 2019-nCoV [coronavirus], European
countries have the necessary capacities to prevent and control
an outbreak as soon as cases are detected". On television the
president of the authoritative Robert Koch Institute in Berlin
described the danger as "minimal". Those reassuring words
were founded on the World Health Organization's assessment
– based on Chinese data and maintained for a long time – that
there was "no or limited human-to-human transmission".

Meanwhile Beijing took strong measures. As early as 22
January, just before celebrations of Chinese New Year, the
authorities sealed off the epicentre of infection, Wuhan.
The world watched in astonishment as China constructed a
thousand-bed hospital in a matter of ten days. It was revealing, however, that the European public saw this formidable

decisiveness mainly as Asiatic collectivism and diligence, not the response to a disaster that was relentlessly heading towards it.

Danger signals did not get through. In governmental public health circles, concern rapidly increased, especially when on 30 January 2020 the WHO declared the situation a "public health emergency of international concern". Alarm among experts who had recently experienced epidemics of respiratory diseases like SARS reached health ministers, who were the first responsible politicians to be warned. But they did not convert the signals into powerful messages within their governments or to the public at large.

Typical was the half-hearted response by the Council of the 27 EU health ministers. They share hardly any projects or responsibilities (unlike their colleagues in agriculture or finance), since public health is a national competence. Consequently they had not formed a tight community; the required European coordination had previously been dealt with in meetings held every six months. That the ministers met urgently on 13 February highlighted that something was up, something that affected them all.* Their meeting was the Union's first visible, political response to the epidemic, but no sense of urgency emanated from it.

Even the run-up to the meeting was messy. The Croatian minister whose country held the six-month chairmanship of the Council had been in his job for only two weeks, Prime Minister Plenkovic having sacked his predecessor in late January. Exhortations to consult quickly – from Brussels by

---

* The treaty article in question, however modest, offers an opening for Union action in the case of "major health scourges" and "combating serious cross-border threats to health" (Art. 168, para. 1, TFEU).

health commissioner Stella Kyriakides, from Rome by minister Robert Speranza, from Paris by Agnès Buzyn and her German colleague Jens Spahn[2] – hit a brick wall in Zagreb.* This blocking of a sense of urgency can also be detected in the tame declaration put together by the 27 ministers in Brussels. The focus was on the outside world: aid for China and other countries affected, plus measures concerning international airline traffic. The latter did not go far, involving merely voluntary questionnaires for passengers arriving from China.[3] As for internal preparations, the director of the EU agency for infectious diseases was able to tell the ministers that there were no problems with the testing capacity needed to keep a possible outbreak under control. Few media made any mention of the meeting.

Underestimation tripped up the authorities almost everywhere in the world, but those of Europe in particular. To the European public, infectious diseases were either historical (medieval plague, cholera, Spanish influenza) or exotic (leprosy and ebola in Africa, SARS, MERS, and now Covid-19 in Asia).[4] So existing scenarios for a disruptive outbreak of flu that were lying ready in countless ministries and think tanks were not translated into decisions. Help for other countries was the first reflex; the public and politicians had experience with that.

---

* Regrettable too was that mere days after this Council meeting, Buzyn was forced to step down. As an authoritative doctor, professor and medical administrator, the French politician might have been able to prompt a more decisive approach by the unaccustomed ministerial circle, but President Macron decreed that she must stand for the mayoralty of Paris, after his chosen candidate withdrew as the result of a sexting scandal. "I wept", Buzyn told *Le Monde* shortly afterwards about leaving her ministry, "because I knew a tsunami was heading towards us".

Although the Brussels inner sphere shared that insouciance, there was also the inconvenience that other crises had not yet blown themselves out or been resolved. In the political economy of media attention, ongoing and familiar stories are the focus. In late January, when the commissioners for public health and crisis management, Stella Kyriakides and Janesz Lenarcic, announced that an internal crisis mechanism was being activated, hardly anyone was in the room. The Brussels press corps was reporting on the imminent Brexit. In mid-February a summit of government leaders concerning the European budget took place, which demanded preambles, reports and, afterwards, explanations of its inglorious failure. In early March, when the coronavirus was already shaking Italy, Turkey's President Erdoğan sent Syrian and Afghan refugees to his country's western border in buses. The presidents of the European Council, Commission and Parliament – Michel, von der Leyen and Sassoli – hurried to the Greek/Turkish border on 3 March in the company of Greek prime minister Mitsotakis, with a convoy of press in their wake. Greece, according to von der Leyen's martial message, was "the shield of Europe". The generals were fighting the previous war.

The virus seemed no threat when far away, nor when it arrived at the door, nor even when it first got inside. Only when SARS-CoV-2 started to do what the coronavirus family has done for centuries, multiplying rapidly, only when its exponential course was further propelled by a Europe-wide Carnival holiday with its many processions, by public feasting, skiing holidays, football matches (Atalanta Bergamo vs Valencia was a "biological bomb", as the mayor of the northern Italian city later admitted) and other mass gatherings large and small, did the authorities stir into action.

On Sunday 23 February northern Italy closed off 11 districts and Bergamo became known as the "Italian Wuhan". Chaos spread through the region's hospitals, which had few ventilators. Doctors and nurses were "sent out like firefighters in pyjamas".[5] People were dying in hospital corridors. On 28 February Rome submitted an official request for medical support from its European partners.

Gasping for breath

At the moment Italy appealed for help – face masks, protective equipment, ventilators – the other member states realized this disaster could hit them too, and immediately. That was when governmental panic hit. Suddenly Covid-19 was no longer an exotic illness but on the doorstep and neighbours gasping for breath were left to their fate. Act now to save yourselves.

On 3 March the French government requisitioned all supplies of face masks and medical protective equipment on its territory, and all relevant production lines. It introduced a maximum price for disinfectant soap. The next day, Germany banned the export of precisely those products, even to other EU member states. These were gross infringements of EU rules by the two most powerful members of the club.

Three days later, at an emergency meeting in Brussels, the health ministers quarrelled about access to personal protective equipment (PPE). This time the media were fascinated. Belgian minister Maggie De Block, whose country is dependent on imports, complained about a "flagrant" breach of solidarity, "contrary to the European spirit".[6] The Commission, in the person of internal market commissioner Thierry

Breton, reprimanded Paris and Berlin. German minister Jens Spahn, under fire, used the many infections in his country as an excuse but was prepared to reconsider his national export ban, as long as the Commission introduced a Europe-wide ban with respect to the rest of the world. The recently appointed Olivier Véran smoothed over France's raw nationalism, but promised no one any supplies. The coronavirus was a public matter, but a French one.[7]

Meanwhile, ten days after its cry for help, Italy had still not received any medical aid from the Union, as its ambassador to the EU divulged: "Unfortunately, not a single EU country responded to the Commission's call. Only China responded bilaterally. Certainly, this is not a good sign of European solidarity".[8] Yet at the video summit of government leaders later that day – the first ever – France, Germany and the Czech Republic stuck to their ban. It was not until 15 March, "after intense discussions" between the Commission, Paris and Berlin, that exports of medical equipment to Italy were restored, as a relieved Commissioner Breton reported on Twitter. By then the damage had been done. European solidarity is dead, the press and public concluded.

In the vacuum left by the politicians, the sense of community and solidarity were saved in those days by local and regional initiatives. In border areas, intensive care units took Covid patients from hospitals over the border. Eleven Italian patients were treated in Austria, 85 in Germany. Dutch hospitals transferred 58 patients to western Germany. Patients from France's badly hit eastern region went to Luxembourg (11), Germany (130) and Austria (3). The Czech Republic too, not a neighbour, expressed a willingness to take French patients. Doctors and nurses from Romania helped out in Milan and

Bergamo. This was European solidarity without central management or institutional form.

Or could "Europe" do something after all and, away from its arbitrage role of admonition and exhortation, entering the field, involve itself in the fight for life-saving face masks? That was the other path the Commission trod after the Italian distress signal, in a fit of rules-politics overconfidence. The Union has no stockpiles or factories as such, so it would have to be a matter of purchase. On 28 February the Commission published a public tender for face masks and PPE. In the emergency procedure, manufacturers were given six days to sign up. But not a single company put in a bid.[9] A few days later a Chinese aircraft landed in Rome with 30 tons of medical supplies "made in China".

On 17 March the Commission put out a second call, this time for gloves, masks, eye protection and overalls. "A success", reported von der Leyen a week later with pride. Enough reliable bids had come in to furnish all interested member states with the supplies asked for. Her message was: this is EU solidarity in action; membership pays off; Italy, Spain – Europe is coming to the rescue![10] Yet the trucks did not set off immediately. There was some small print. The equipment would not be available until two weeks after signature of the contract with the producers, depending on (per a footnote to the press release) "the offers, the production capacity of the companies and delivery time needed as well as the specifications of the contracts". Mid-April at the earliest, then. Rapid by bureaucratic standards, but agonizingly slow in a life-and-death crisis. We need more speed, government leaders told von der Leyen on 26 March.[11] In their own countries the hospitals were stretched to breaking point in a desperate fight for life. Nursing homes were still operating under the political radar.

In a pandemic the laws of a wartime economy apply, not those of a market economy. There is suddenly no longer a market for face masks or test kits in which you can invite tenders. It is not the balance between supply and demand expressed in a price that determines who gets what, but instead the balance of power, the capacity of a state to demand, produce, plunder if necessary, or, in a variant partially in line with market forces, to use soft pressure to set up direct contacts between industry and buyers. American president Trump (who invoked a law from the Korean War to force General Motors to produce medical ventilators) intuited as much immediately, as did his French counterpart Macron. Xi in Beijing and Putin in Moscow work that way in any case. Anyone unwilling or unable to permit themselves such brutal power politics needs to do more for countless millions of face masks than put together a competent procurement advert. What remained of the market in PPE in the spring of 2020 was a jungle of nocturnal deals and extortionate prices.

Whereas the larger of the member states, when they finally faced up to the threat to public health, increased their speed of action and their political forcefulness, the Brussels institutions did not have such a change of course available to them. In itself that was no great problem. The difficulty arises when the specialists in rules, appraisals and criteria believe themselves capable of tackling a refugee crisis by means of asylum quotas, as they had five years earlier, or of fine-tuning an acute pandemic by means of tendering procedures. Overconfidence in rules-politics leads to practical debacles and – especially if you are posing as a lifesaver – to a loss of public trust.

Stockpiles and vaccines

Planning and programming comes more easily to the Commission than acting in the panicky present. It quickly drew lessons for the future from the disaster. Never again should shortages of medical equipment cost lives. So it was a matter of laying in supplies as buffers against future shocks. The decision was official by 19 March.[12]

From granaries in ancient Egypt to Roman water towers, strategic supplies are *res publica* in optima forma, material monuments to the public cause. But how does that work in practice? The European Union is not a state, the Commission is not a federal government – unlike the US federal government, visibly present in 50 states. Joint responsibility takes shape in revealingly hybrid forms, in an interplay between Brussels and the member states, on the boundary between rules-politics and events-politics.

The Union's new stockpiles of medical equipment (ventilators, protective clothing, laboratory supplies) were warehoused and managed by member states. Germany and Romania were the first to report for duty. They would hold the stocks and also be responsible for contracting, purchase and distribution. For its part, the Commission would finance acquisition, storage and transport. With €50 million available, the plan was put into operation.

Financier is a modest role, but not a superfluous one. In Belgium health minister De Block came under fire in March 2020 when the press discovered that she had caused a strategic stockpile of six million face masks, bought by the Belgian state at the time of the Mexican flu, to be destroyed in 2018 and had not replaced them, a casualty of cutbacks when the rental contract for the barracks in question expired.

Since the start of the pandemic the Commission has also used the EU budget to support emergency medical transport. Anyone who moved supplies, medical teams or patients between member countries would have their expenses reimbursed. This was a new budgetary instrument, a formal embedding of the solidarity between hospitals in border regions seen in the spring of 2020. Such a division of roles is tailored to fit constitutional relationships within the Union, but the money lever brings limitations of its own. Strategic stockpiles are intended for times of crisis and it is precisely then – as in the battle over face masks – that not everything can be achieved with money alone.

Just as the Covid outbreak unleashed a worldwide pursuit of personal protective equipment, so the members states invested as much as possible in the development of a vaccine, as the best chance of salvation from the pandemic and as a power factor that could be deployed in the rough-and-tumble world of trade and geo-medical politics.

On this front too, the Union placed its faith in its financial firepower, and not without success. A donor conference organized by the Commission in May 2020 after a call from the WHO brought in pledges worth almost €16 billion. Three quarters were from public treasuries in the Union, whether governments or EU institutions. Vaccine development is the task of commercial pharmaceutical laboratories, but with advance purchasing agreements – investment in research in return for guaranteed acquisition in case of success – the authorities could take a direct share in businesses that provide for the health of their peoples. *Res publica.*

No herd

The most far-reaching public-health-political decision was made by European societies very soon after the outbreak began: to lock down. For lack of vaccines or treatments, the virus would have to be suppressed by means of "non-pharmaceutical interventions", in other words by changing society's behaviour. Timing, intensity and conviction differed, but the main thrust was the same. Personal freedom must be limited in order to prevent a collapse of the healthcare system. Italy set the tone, both with the spectre of chaos in hospitals and with its robust response. On 9 March 2020 it locked down the entire country.

For a short time a few European states sought a less drastic way out, the UK foremost among them, joined by the Netherlands and Sweden. They were guided by two notions. Firstly, advisors to the British government did not believe the public would put up with strict measures; they feared "behavioural fatigue" and therefore did not want to start too soon. Secondly, there was a belief in London, The Hague and Stockholm that it was unnecessary to stop the virus completely, given that those who survived it would gain immunity. Consequently, mitigation would suffice, keeping the prevalence of illness down to a level that would not overwhelm hospitals and intensive care units. The notion of "herd immunity" did not persist for long, however. In mid-March researchers at Imperial College in London calculated that the death toll with an optimal mitigation strategy would be extremely high, while the likelihood of reaching herd immunity would still be very limited. Eight times the number of intensive-care beds available in the British hospital system would be needed, with 260,000 deaths forecast as a consequence. The scientists therefore advised that for countries able to implement it, suppression of the virus was the preferred policy option.[13] In response to this sobering analysis, the British government changed course. The dire remedy of a lockdown was all that remained.

So all European societies (with one or two exceptions) opted for the maximum protection of individual lives – irrespective of the impact, initially. A revealing choice as regards the values of the continent, and one with far-reaching consequences both for societies individually and for their Union. Because whatever variety of lockdown was imposed, tens of millions of people all over Europe would be forced to stay at home, unable to go to work, unable to spend money in shops or restaurants and unable to travel. So in this first Act the multifarious national public health crisis also, indeed above all, entailed a border crisis and a debt crisis. In the former the Union falteringly made a number of discoveries; the latter would transform it.

BORDERS

(23 FEBRUARY–1 SEPTEMBER 2020)

On Sunday 23 February the lockdown began in 11 northern Italian municipalities. That same evening, Austria halted a train travelling from Venice to Munich because of two possibly infected passengers. The rail border was shut for several hours. In Lyon the next morning the French police surrounded a night bus from Milan because the driver had a suspicious cough. By Monday reporters in Brussels were raising questions about

Schengen.[14] Closing borders against infection was "dispro-portionate and ineffective", the health ministers of Italy and eight neighbouring countries declared at a meeting in Rome on 25 February. The EU agency for infectious diseases and, a week later, the European commissioner for crisis management backed them up.[15] Nevertheless, further reports appeared about ad hoc coronavirus checks at airports and border cross-ings. On 11 March Austria became the first to close a national border against the virus, its border with Italy.

The real blow came when on 15 March Germany announced it was closing its borders with France, Austria, Switzerland, Denmark and Luxembourg as of the following morning. A remarkable decision. Even at the height of the refugee crisis in 2015, the Federal Republic, in contrast to many other mem-ber states, had refrained from such a measure, in fact keeping the border open had been a source of pride. "Goodbye Schen-gen" was the headline in the Italian business newspaper *Il Sole 24 Ore* the next day. A 60-kilometre queue of trucks on the border with Poland, after comparable measures by Warsaw, made a great impression on the German public.

Within Schengen, member states can decide to close their borders on grounds of public safety or public health.[16] Clo-sures need to be proportional to the threat, temporary and evidence-based, of course, but the pandemic emergency had no patience with any questions raised. The Commission was able to smooth some rough edges. On 16 March it advocated exceptions for border workers and citizens stranded outside their own countries, and urged that borders be kept open for the transport of essential goods, especially medicines and food. It also proposed closing Europe's external borders, and the government leaders agreed to that at their video summit the next day.[17] Perhaps cordoning off the outside world might help to make controls on the internal borders less arbitrary.

Yet barriers being raised hit the Union hard; this was much more symbolic and visible than the battle for face masks. Although a lack of action in the field of public health can be justified in a formal sense (no competence), the same does not apply to freedom of movement, a concrete achievement the Union likes to brag about. It was an open goal for journalists, who all too quickly concluded from the return of internal border controls, as they had in 2015, that the end of Schengen and the Union was nigh.[18] In *The Guardian* a young Italian law professor staying in Spain spoke of the end of the European dream: "After two decades of virtually unconditional border-free movement, millions of us are currently feeling estrangement and loss".[19]

Such assessments lacked a sense of proportion. In Italy and Spain people were shut up in their houses in the spring of 2020, while in France citizens were forced to remain within one kilometre of home. In the context of such restrictions on freedom, the inconvenience of a closed national border fades to near insignificance. As a public health emergency measure, the (nationally imposed) restriction on freedom of movement trumped the (European) right to freedom of movement between member states. It was unfortunate for people who cross the internal borders almost daily – and in financial trading post Luxembourg there were more of them than in spacious and remote Finland – but it was hardly the end of European civilization.

A patchwork quilt

If at the start the Union could do little more than ride the waves of the pandemic and use its considerable power to seal itself off, it was not long before – in the video conference of 26 March to be precise – government leaders were asking the Commission for an exit strategy. Movement in the opposite direction, towards opening up, must be more orderly. On 13 May, following a mid-April interim report, president von der Leyen made an announcement about the restoration of free movement and removal of border controls.[20]

As the state of emergency in the hospitals eased, European governments increasingly sought new strategies to give shape to a defensible balance between economic and health priorities. At what cost to health would schools, offices, sports clubs and restaurants be allowed to reopen? And at what economic cost was society prepared to block the spread of the virus? The same dilemma applied to national borders. Closure was expensive, and a violation of freedom, whereas opening up inevitably meant losing control of the spread of the virus. While European goods transport was largely immune to border closures, restrictions on travel brought tourism more or less to a standstill. Tourism accounts for a tenth of the Union's prosperity and an eighth of its jobs, even more in the South, first to be hit by the pandemic. The first objective of politicians and policy-makers was to keep the internal borders open. "This summer we will be among Europeans", President Macron told the French in early May.

For tourists and travellers, the map of Europe became a patchwork quilt. Green, yellow, orange, red – in fluctuating, virus-induced patterns. Some member states closed all their

borders, others none. Some demanded quarantine or a negative test on return, others did not. Member states in the East,
which were keeping the virus rather better under control during this first wave, formed open-border groups. From mid-May
the "Baltic bubble" announced a travel space for citizens of
Estonia, Latvia and Lithuania, and in early June Poland joined
it.[21] But those who shut in, also shut out. Denmark and Norway opened their shared border on 1 June, but their Covid-
lax neighbour Sweden was explicitly excluded; Sweden's foreign minister deplored this "political decision".[22] In late May
Greece, craving tourists, announced it would open its borders on 15 June to citizens of all EU countries except Italy and
Spain, prompting the Italian vice-premier to fulminate that
his country did not wish to be treated as a "leper colony".[23]

These choices and clashes were a challenge to the Brussels
doctrine of free movement of people. First of all, they put the
basic principle of non-discrimination under strain. The Commission would have preferred to see the borders closed either
to residents of all EU member states (if it was indeed necessary) or to none. That way nobody would be discriminated
against. The actual situation was a messy halfway house, however, with access given to residents of some member states
or regions and not to others. This could be defended, as long
as it was done based on epidemiological criteria, but disturb-
ingly, geography was involved. The Estonian foreign minister
drily described the expansion of the Baltic bubble by saying,
"If we look at the map, Poland is important for our people as a
transit corridor".[24] Whereas the Brussels rule-making factory
traditionally wishes away, as far as possible, the unique spatial position and historical experience of member states, the
coronavirus brought a minor revenge of geography.

Secondly, the pandemic hammered away at the sacred quartet of freedom of movement: goods, capital, services and people. Economic interests meant that goods transport was discreetly given the green light, whereas the transport of people was stopped because it posed a greater risk to health. (Digital movement of capital does not cause infection and nobody was talking about services.) It was a justifiable distinction given the situation, put forward by the Commission. Yet eyebrows will have been raised in London. It amounted to the negation of a point the Union had insisted was non-negotiable before and after the British referendum of 2016, namely that the Union's four freedoms were inseparable as pillars of Europe as a civilized space, so that no exception could be made for the movement of people. Now, ironically just two months after the British departure, it proved possible after all.*

The inner world of Brussels reacted to the pandemic border shocks in the old-fashioned way. A taboo from the years of its foundation came to the fore. The reintroduction of border controls was automatically seen as a return of war or dictatorship. As European Commissioner for Home Affairs Ylva Johansson put it to the Parliament in early May, "It's like travelling in a time machine to a dark and distant past. We now need to get back to the future. Back to normality".[25] The border as relic. In 1953, as chair of the forerunner to the Commission, Jean Monnet was handed the first European *laissez-passer*. During the ceremony in Luxembourg he asked a member of staff for his French passport and said, "We're going to burn this now".[26] That was then. We now know that even after 70 years

---

* Important distinction: the UK had always asked for a permanent exception to be made for itself alone, whereas in the pandemic it was a matter of a temporary exception for all.

of European integration, national borders have not become meaningless lines on the map but remain a basis for the practical and symbolic organization of the political, economic and social life of member states. We would do well to take full account of that fact.

In mid-June most of the internal borders of the Union were unlocked again. As one of the last, the border between Portugal and Spain was opened two weeks later. On Wednesday 1 July there were solemn celebrations in the border towns of Badajoz (Spain) and Elvas (Portugal). Ceremonies were presided over by Spain's King Felipe VI and attended by Portugal's President Marcelo Rebelo de Sousa and both prime ministers, Pedro Sanchez and António Costa. All the guests had lunch on the Spanish side and an aperitif on the Portuguese side.

In the Europe of summer 2020 this festively restored unity and freedom of movement proved short-lived. Whereas the "fatigue" of behavioural science was vigorously thrust aside at the start of the lockdown – a combination of moral appeal, civic responsibility and fear proved stronger than the models had reckoned on – at this point it made itself felt. Infection figures rose again in the autumn, especially where large numbers of people were living close together without protection.

External borders

One of the most successful improvisations during the crisis – right at the start – concerned the repatriation of Europeans stranded all over the globe. Countries like Germany and the Netherlands felt that if they were bringing citizens from India or Australia home, they might as well take a few Italians or Slovenes with them. No EU planes were needed, only the sharing of information plus some money and goodwill.* Combined diplomatic and logistical efforts – coordinated by a taskforce rapidly put together by the EU diplomatic service – brought more than half a million EU citizens home in the early weeks, quite a job given the Covid travel restrictions imposed all over the world. A joint capacity to act, deployed at the crucial moment – for once the self-congratulation was justified.[27] The readiness of the Union to care for people was a clear signal to all its citizens.

The attachment to the open internal borders forced joint action in respect of the outside world. On paper this is an obvious deduction; in the pandemic, despite considerable counterpressure, it was visibly implemented for the first time.

The litmus test was how the EU handled the United States, the country of origin of millions of business visitors and tourists every year, which had a thoroughly ineffective coronavirus policy. The European public felt insulted when on 12 March President Trump unexpectedly banned all travel between the US and Schengen. What, us? A few months later the roles were reversed. Europe had the pandemic under control, as did China and other Asian countries, but in the US it was gathering pace. On 1 July, two weeks after the internal borders were unlocked, the Union opened its external borders to a first group of countries, which did not include the US. The *New York Times* called this travel ban "a stinging blow to American prestige in the world".[28] Residents of Putin's Russia, Bolsonaro's Brazil and Erdoğan's Turkey were equally unwelcome in the EU.

---

* This was placed in a legal framework without difficulty as a result of the treaty article specifying that citizens of member states have a right to consular protection from another member state if their own state does not or cannot represent them in a country outside the EU (art. 23, TFEU).

A travel ban is onerous. It jeopardizes diplomatic relations. It expresses distrust, as Trump's ban in March had done: your citizens present a danger to ours. Such a measure is not introduced lightly. So Brussels chose objective criteria, such as the 14-day average of new infections. Even so, hours of diplomatic consultation were required before an agreement between ambassadors of all EU member states could be reached. Travellers from 15 countries were given the green light, including Australia, Canada, Morocco, Serbia and Thailand.

It is fascinating to see how all the member states' assessments of the requirements of the economy as against public health came together in decisions about the EU's external border. A revelation. The question of whom to let in takes you in a single step from epidemiological advice to foreign policy, from WHO laboratories and the Robert Koch Institute to the way of thinking of Henry Kissinger and *Foreign Affairs*. Thus a political order experiences itself as a body politic because it shares an external border. The skin is a sensitive organ. Conversely, anyone who draws up their own border plan is saying, I am not part of you.

A sixteenth country was on the green list: China. Chinese citizens were allowed to come to the European Union from 1 July onwards, but on condition of reciprocity. And China still thought Europe too infectious.

All things considered, the politics of the European borders had not yet managed to get to grips with the pandemic. The event therefore stretched farther out in time. The list for the external border was reviewed every two weeks, that breakthrough held, but work on the internal borders was more problematic. In the autumn of 2020, the German EU Council presidency made diligent efforts to coordinate the patchwork of colours and measures, but everyone realized that a new wave of Covid might lead to a reimposition of border controls. Because of insufficient testing and tracing capacity, Europe had not yet succeeded in tracking all new infections back to a single patient, to one cluster of a family, choir or wedding, nor even one district, village, city or region. Until enough people had been inoculated with some kind of vaccine, health politics would mean the disciplining of healthy citizens, and national borders would serve as health borders – with all the inevitable consequences.

DEBT AND CREDIT
(9 MARCH–21 JULY 2020)

On Monday 9 March 2020, when Italy became the first country in the world to put its entire territory into lockdown, Covid panic broke out on the financial markets. Share prices plummeted in Asia, Europe and America. The DAX in Frankfurt had its worst day since the terror attacks of 2001, US and UK stock markets since the 2008 banking crisis. Investors are never scared off by risks and fluctuations – gambling on the future is after all their profession – but the coronavirus brought too much uncertainty. It was clear, at the very least, that a worldwide recession as a consequence of the pandemic lockdowns would hit the European economy hard.[29]

As soon as the pandemic began to affect economic activity and employment – following on from public health and freedom of movement – a different cast stepped onto the political stage. For global coordination the leading actors are the IMF and the World Bank, the monetary counterparts of the WHO.

At a European level the 27 finance ministers set to work with the European commissioners; unlike their colleagues in public health and in justice and home affairs, they form a tight and resolute group. The dynamic also changed the distribution of roles, as public expectations rose and political tensions increased. Very soon the government leaders were expected to take the stage.

After the market panic of 9 March, the spotlight shone first on the guardian of the single currency, the European Central Bank. Since 2008 the institution has gained authority as the tamer of crises. In the state of emergency it developed an unconventional and unexpected vigour, stepping out of its straitjacket of rules-politics. The markets recalled the bold promise of President Mario Draghi that it would do "whatever it takes" to save the euro (2012). What could the Bank do in this calamity?

It began with an instructive error. On 12 March the ECB decided on a package of measures including a €120 billion asset purchasing programme. Careless words from bank president Christine Lagarde, recently appointed, negated the effect. At a press conference she said "we are not here to close spreads".[30] So if the interest rate in, say, Italy rose, that was a matter for other bodies. Lagarde also distanced herself from the resolute approach of her predecessor ("I don't have a claim to history for being 'whatever-it-takes' number two"). With this crack in the defences, the markets knew what to do. Immediately after the press conference, Italian interest rates rose. *Come se ciò non bastasse!* – as if it wasn't enough already! From Rome the Italian head of state chided that in this hour of need, "at least in the common interest" he expected "initiatives of solidarity" and not "moves that can hinder their action".[31] A week later, by which time a good many eurozone countries were in lockdown and the skies were darkening, the response came up to the mark. On 18 March the ECB decided on a pandemic package of €750 billion.[32] The aim was to quell speculation about the disintegration of the eurozone. This time the markets responded positively. In an explanatory blog, Lagarde wrote that this intervention would, if necessary, be only the start, both in size and in length: "We will explore all options and all contingencies to support the economy through this shock".[33] Your central bank is at your service.

Nonetheless, monetary policy hit its limits during the pandemic. In 2012 Draghi's message to speculators was, "you can't destroy the euro, our will is stronger", but in the Covid crisis such rhetorical bluff could not work. The weak spot concerned not faith in the future but bodily resilience. After all, the attack came not from self-fulfilling prophecies of doom but from a self-replicating virus. So the precise equivalent in the pandemic of Draghi's "whatever it takes", the promise to act as lender of last resort, was the availability of a vaccine or treatment – a remedy of last resort.

When as a consequence of the lockdowns supply (production) and demand (consumption) collapsed simultaneously, financial reassurance (liquidity) was not enough. So as well as the central bank, it was now also, indeed primarily, up to the governments with their budgetary policies. That is what Lagarde with her nonchalant and ambiguous words on 12 March – which one French expert claimed were deliberate[34] – had intended to say: over to you.[35]

The lockdown forced all European governments to draw on their own treasuries immediately, and hugely. Companies were given state support, employees paid to stay at home, bank guarantees provided or prolonged, deferred payment permitted. Even Berlin shook off an old obsession with balancing the budget.[36] But what could and should European governments and institutions do together, with, or for each other?

One thing was achieved immediately. For a start, the Union must allow individual states to act separately, by suspending restrictive rules. This happened without any problem and more quickly than during the banking crisis of 2008. The EU institutions were willing to "use all the necessary and possible flexibilities for these exceptional circumstances", said von der Leyen as early as 9 March.[37] Necessity knows no law. The Commission stretched the state aid criteria, allowing governments to help their industries. When it came to limits on budgetary deficits and national debt, it advocated using "escape clauses".[38] Amid all the pandemic misery, nobody wanted to experience "Brussels" as onerous. Do not get in the way, was the starting point. The dilemmas to which this leniency with regard to state action would lead could wait.

But what about combined budgetary clout? On 16 March the finance ministers of the eurozone countries had their first Covid consultation, by video call. Their non-eurozone colleagues joined them.[39] Chair Mario Centeno said afterwards, "We will protect our citizens and our currency come what may and with everything we have got". Promising words. The conclusion drawn from an inventory by the Commission and the European Investment Bank was that from the existing EU money pots, a modest €100 billion was available as emergency aid to governments and businesses.[40] Too paltry, the government leaders agreed. On 26 March, during their third video summit in three weeks, leaders asked finance ministers to do their homework again within a fortnight, taking account of the "unprecedented nature of the Covid-19 shock affecting all our countries".[41] The latter is code for: this disaster is nobody's fault, take action now.

On a side stage, the fat was in the fire. In a video meeting earlier in the week, the Dutch finance minister Wopke Hoekstra had astonished his colleagues with a request that the Commission put together a report with recommendations regarding why some member states lacked "financial buffers". Surely they could have saved in good times for bad times to come? Totally lacking in empathy, it was a question to which everyone already knew the answer, asked at a moment when Italy, Spain and France were losing hundreds of citizens to Covid every day. All the resentment and anger in Southern Europe about the euro crisis welled up and swamped the arrogant financial experts of the North. After a quarrelsome video summit on 26 March, the Portuguese prime minister António Costa called Hoekstra's words "repugnant". "No one wants to hear another Dutch finance minister say what was said in 2009, 2010 and 2011".[42] The Hague regretted the commotion but, like Berlin, continued to oppose unconditional emergency financing and joint debt.

In this tense situation, in the early morning of 9 April, after a video session lasting more than 16 hours, the finance ministers reached a major agreement. The French and German ministers Bruno Le Maire and Olaf Scholz brought North and South together as spokespeople for each camp. To get Hoekstra on board, Macron and Merkel had to ring his boss Rutte in The Hague at dawn.[43] The result was the creation of three European shock absorbers, amounting to €540 billion in total: a pandemic credit line of €240 billion from the stability mechanism for the costs of medical care and prevention,

€200 billion in bank guarantees for businesses, and €100 billion in loans for wage subsidies. With the latter the Union as a whole was stepping onto the terrain of welfare support, not as a first port of call (it remains a national competence) but as a safety net for the states. Partial unemployment, or *Kurzarbeit*, first tried in 2008, proved effective once again. While in the US around 22 million people lost their jobs in March and April 2020, in the EU the figure was limited to 640,000.[44] That number would rise, as everyone knew, but the ministers had not yet started to think about a recovery fund for reconstruction after the pandemic.

So with old and new shock absorbers, the Union institutions offered within one month, between the market panic of 9 March and the Maundy Thursday agreement of 9 April, an initial financial response. The speed of action was much greater than in earlier crises. Players now had previous experience to call upon; the ECB discovered it was obliged to display the resolve shown in the previous crisis. Instruments that were not on hand in earlier crises (such as the stability mechanism for the eurozone) were now ready and waiting. Commission and Investment Bank emerged as proficient providers of credit. Domestically the German government threw off its dread of Keynesianism and did not step on the brake in Brussels. And when energy flagged, the public urged stallers and obstructionists to act.

The German chancellor's leap

"In the long run things can go well with Germany only if they go well with Europe". In her 15 years in office, Angela Merkel said something of this kind several times in the Bundestag, but never with more sincerity and conviction than in her first speech to parliament after the start of the pandemic, on Thursday 23 April 2020. To the German parliamentarians – spaced out at a suitable distance, several of them wearing face masks – she declared unequivocally at the opening, "This crisis presents all of us, government and parliament, our entire country with its greatest challenge since the Second World War, since the founding years of the Federal Republic". For that reason, she predicted, "the question of how we prevent the virus at some point overwhelming our health system and costing the lives of countless people as a result will for a long time be the central question for the politicians in Germany and Europe".[45]

The previous evening she had presided over a meeting of all members of the governing coalition to consult on national measures, and several hours after that she had taken part in yet another video summit of the European Council. The German and European perspectives were interwoven in her speech; the Union is a "*Schicksalsgemeinschaft*", a community of destiny. Therefore, Merkel prepared her listeners, Germany will "in the spirit of solidarity" have to provide the EU budget with "a very different, or clearly higher" contribution. A solid recovery fund would be needed to steer all the member states through the pandemic.

The Union creaked and groaned, and Angela Merkel knew the podium was calling. The first shock had been brought under control by mid-April, but the pandemic was a threat to Europe's unity and solidarity. From three sides the federal chancellor felt forces demanding action.

First there was the threat of an economic watershed. Daily she was reading reports of how Covid-19 was driving the

German heart of the eurozone and its Mediterranean periphery apart economically. Northern countries had far more reserves than Southern countries with which to keep companies going and preserve jobs. Germany was pumping more money into its own economy than all the other member states put together (the Commission calculated), more than after the banking crisis, more even than after German unification.[46] That meant there was little left of a level playing field in the internal market. Resentment in the South is easily fed, Merkel realized: the first victims of the virus, then unemployed because of German competition. Moreover, in the economic game of supply and demand, a boomerang effect is never far away. "Europe is our biggest export market and it mustn't be lost", German employers warned. Trade wars with and between America and China were already driving quite enough economic uncertainty.

Secondly, political fault lines were grating and grinding. The discord between North and South – verbal fireworks in public and high-minded exchanges behind the scenes – did not bode well. Wounds from the euro crisis were reopened. Germany can quickly become the bogeyman, as Merkel knew from experience. Although to domestic observers the German chancellor is one of the players, albeit an important one, in a sophisticated balance of power between political institutions, coalition parties and layers of government, to the rest of Europe and the world at large things look rather different: Merkel *is* Germany. During the euro crisis her portrait featured on banners in Athens and magazine covers in Madrid, and in the migrant crisis her name was chanted by Syrian refugees. Charity coincided with reasons of state. In a European life-and-death crisis, Germany must not be seen as the miser on duty.

Then, thirdly, there was France and the perpetual French call for a European marriage of convenience. Since taking office in 2017, Emmanuel Macron had been trying to tempt Angela Merkel into some form of European innovation – defence, digitalization, climate: there was no shortage of initiatives. But his priority was the euro, and on that matter Berlin sent him away empty-handed. There was no shortage of excuses: Because coalition talks... Because public opinion... Because the Constitutional Court... The Paris dream of a budget for the eurozone dwindled under pressure from the Germans and Dutch into a money pot of negligible size, with as its name an acronym easier to forget than to remember (BICC).[47] French frustration resulted.[48] Yet Macron swore to his friend Daniel Cohn-Bendit, in the bar of a hotel in Aachen where he was presented with a European award on Ascension Day in 2018, "*Je ne lâcherai pas*": I won't let it drop.[49]

In the pandemic, the French president spotted fresh chances. He skilfully switched back and forth between acting as a lawyer for the South (who could threaten a breach) and as an indispensable partner to Berlin. Shortly after Easter, Macron brought things to a head publicly in the *Financial Times*. At this historic moment in 2020, Europe must not make the same mistake as in Versailles in 1919, when a defeated Germany was saddled with huge reparations payments. The logic of guilt and punishment must be swept aside, as was the objective of the Marshall Plan after 1945, which enabled West Germany and others to rebuild their countries and economies.[50] The call of history was understood. Like her predecessors Adenauer, Schmidt and Kohl, at this European moment of truth, Merkel sought an entente with the French president.

The monetary union would need to form a bridge between

South and North, a span that connected economies, eased political tensions and authenticated the Franco-German pact. No easy task. Positions on both sides have been fixed for a long time. France once forced through the common currency and allowed the Federal Republic to determine what it would look like. Since then, the basic principle has been a shared currency but one in which the member states remain responsible for their state finances. For each German chancellor, moving away from that principle means a loss of public support and a violation of the constitution (closely guarded by Karlsruhe). It would be both political suicide and constitutional high treason.

The Treaty of Maastricht (1992) includes three barriers to joint liability for individual budgets. The first of them, "no credit facility", or no money tap to turn on, has been tinkered with ever since the euro crisis. In 2010 the ECB in Frankfurt started buying national debt on the secondary markets and Berlin made no move to stop it. The other two barriers, however, held out even in the euro storm. The second is "no transfers", or no money to be moved from one member state to another, and the third is "no joint debt issuance", or no "eurobonds". Two red lines, redder than red. "Not in my lifetime," Merkel insisted at the height of the euro crisis on the subject of eurobonds.[51]

In the pandemic both these remaining taboos came under immense pressure. Eurobonds: not even now? On 25 March, nine government leaders – of Italy, Spain, Portugal, Greece, France, Ireland, Belgium, Luxembourg and Slovenia – wrote a letter to the president of the European Council. They appealed for the issuing of joint debt, soon labelled "corona bonds". A day before a video summit, the call to break a 30-year-old taboo was a provocation to Berlin. No, said Merkel, not even now (and her Dutch and Austrian allies Rutte and Kurz backed her up).[52]

Transfers between member states, gifts from the strong to the weak: not even now? Certainly, since the 2010 euro crisis, emergency funds have flowed to member states in difficulties, but those were loans, to be paid back, and they were given in return for reforms; they were conditional and not free money. But in the pandemic the South railed against this limitation. It was stigmatizing. The Italian government refused, partly under pressure from its nationalist opposition, to call on the stability mechanism's new pandemic credit line. It rejected any new bankers' regime, calling instead for political emancipation.

From April two sentences crept into Merkel's argumentation that created an opening. One was technical: the pandemic was a "symmetrical shock", affecting everyone, unlike the previous "asymmetrical" crises, which hit countries with weak economic stewardship. It was nobody's fault this time, so a gesture could be contemplated. The other was political: "an exceptional situation demands an exceptional method", but – Merkel immediately qualified – limited in time and not as a precedent. A one-off bridge, for this unique moment.

After her speech to the Bundestag and the European video summit of 23 April 2020, Merkel sought a rapprochement with Macron. She wanted a solution. Eurobonds remained out of the question, but the chancellor offered another opening to financial solidarity: let the Commission raise money on the markets. Then Berlin would not have to stand surety for debt paid out to Italy or Spain, and backing would come from the EU budget, in other words from the will of the member states to remain together as a Union. Paris would prefer to see com-munitization, or debt issued by the eurozone countries, but it was happy to accept the offer. With a central debt issue, Ger-many lost control over spending (the reason why in 2010 the task was not entrusted to the Commission[53]), but there was an advantage: the debt would not visibly weigh on the national budget. It resembled the manoeuvre that had allowed Merkel to have the ECB printing presses in Frankfurt do the work of saving the Southern Europeans in the euro crisis, for which the Bundestag refused to sign up on behalf of German taxpayers. This time Merkel could not avoid a visible, budgetary policy remedy, but she farmed it out to the Commission in Brussels. That felt less expensive. The formula suited German federal relationships, too, a diplomat explained to *Le Monde* after-wards: "We are used to such a framework. Bavaria, for example, does not pay for the State of Bremen; the federal government takes care of such things".[54]

Furthermore, Merkel was willing to make the financing available entirely in the form of grants. She surprised those around her, and perhaps even herself, with this inference from the "exceptional situation". But how much should be given? While in Rome and Madrid sums of €1,500 or even €2,000 billion were doing the rounds, in its talks with Berlin, Paris brought the relief fund back to acceptable proportions. It was the German chancellor herself who, after much discussion and thorough consideration, committed to the amount in the final weekend of negotiations: €500 billion it must be, in donations alone.

On Monday 18 May a self-aware, almost cheerful Merkel, along with the French president, presented by video – she in Berlin, he in Paris – the plan for a coronavirus recovery fund of €500 billion, to be financed by issuing central debt. The river had been crossed.

A *unanimous agreement*

Within a few days German public opinion moved with the federal chancellor surprisingly quickly. President of the Bundestag Wolfgang Schäuble, as minister of finance the bogeyman of Southern Europe for years, gave a speech in favour of European solidarity as being in Germany's own interests. He settled the debate about the form of financing biblically: loans (which weigh upon the national debt) instead of grants would be "stones in place of bread".[55] The Greeks must have been awestruck. In Merkel's CDU the recovery fund was given a warm reception. Coalition partner the SPD, involved in the plan through finance minister Olaf Scholz, joined in the welcome. In the Bundestag the liberal FDP, opposition voice of the prudent taxpayer, praised the strict budgetary policy, "which means Germany is now in a position to help others".

To parry major shocks in Europe and launch groundbreaking initiatives, Franco–German agreement is necessary, but not sufficient. Partners need to be convinced, and the whole thing embedded in common structures. Even a dual initiative can perish, as Paris and Berlin have seen, to their cost, in the recent past, after their performance in "Deauville" for example.*

In Commission president Ursula von der Leyen, Merkel and Macron have found the indispensable third person of the team.

---

* For this euro crisis episode, see the section "Improvisation" in Chapter 4.

Only the Commission can make a formal proposal and thus guide the plan into the frameworks of rules-politics. The institution also provides expertise. A senior Brussels civil servant, a Dutchman no less, had thought up the revolutionary lending model of joint debt securities back in March. Via von der Leyen, for years a minister in Merkel's cabinets, the idea made its way to Berlin.[56] In the video summit of 23 April, the government leaders asked the Commission president to work out the details of a recovery fund. She was given half-ironic advice by Merkel: "Ursula, don't forget to consult with us".[57] The Commission advocated coupling the coronavirus recovery fund with the seven-year EU budget (2021–27). This placed the institution at the centre of reconstruction after the pandemic. For different reasons, government leaders and summit chair Charles Michel also saw the usefulness of this coupling. The failure of the budgetary summit of 20–21 February 2020 suddenly seemed a blessing in disguise. After all, the more open issues and problems there were, the more chance of trade-offs and buy-offs, and so of an agreement.

It was immediately clear where the opposition lay: in the North. While Southern Europe had wanted more but was satisfied with the Franco-German plan and Merkel's gesture, the Northern allies felt passed over. Shortly after 18 May, the Netherlands, Austria, Denmark and Sweden made a counter-proposal. The "frugal four" clung to the orthodoxy: no grants, only loans, and with proper supervision.[58] Italy is little trusted. At the same time they recognized the power relationships. The movement set going by Merkel could not be stopped, at best it might be curbed or adjusted.

On Wednesday 27 May 2020, Ursula von der Leyen officially launched the Commission's plan for a coronavirus recovery fund in the European Parliament. The commissioner for economy, Italian former minister Paolo Gentilone, robbed her of a scoop on Twitter: the institution was advocating a fund of €750 billion. On top of €500 billion in the form of grants, in accordance with the Merkel–Macron initiative, would come €250 billion in loans, all of it raised on the markets and placed at the disposal of member states hardest hit by the pandemic. Added to the revised proposal for the seven-year budget launched at the same time (in which the sum for public health was 20 times that of the initial 2018 proposal), this meant an injection of €1,800 billion into the European economy, spread over seven years.

On 19 June government leaders had their first video summit since April, and they were hoping it would be their last. Borders were opening, countries were creeping out of their lockdowns and all the players realized that an agreement on billions cannot be settled on screen. Only a physical meeting – where you look each other in the eye, hear the timbre of voices, taste the atmosphere, smell the fear, call the bluff – can bridge differences and lead to unanimous agreement. Council President Charles Michel announced a physical consultation for 17 July.

In sight of the finish, face masks at the ready, everyone visited everyone else. Giuseppe Conte received or went to see no fewer than nine colleagues, Mark Rutte, his Northern counterpart, eight. Merkel received Macron and Conte at Schloss Meseberg and then, in Berlin, Sanchez, Rutte and the Finnish and Polish prime ministers among others. She was the spiritual mother of the agreement and, from 1 July, leader of the rotating presidency of the Council of the EU (which would have to clear through the Parliament any agreement among leaders at ministerial level). The national leaders organized themselves into groups: the frugal quartet, the Visegrád four, the Baltic trio. From Brussels, Michel made video calls with them all. It was a diplomatic ballet across the full width of the stage, catching the public's attention partly through the new demands made of the body language of greeting: what gestures were replacing the handshake and the hug?[59]

As for content, three Covid fund battlefields emerged. First there was the balance between grants and loans. The addition by the Commission of €250 billion in loans over and above the €500 billion in grants may have increased the total sum (an outcome unattractive to the frugal opposition) but it also introduced an additional variable into the game. Then there were the criteria for allocation, being a mixture of level of prosperity, unemployment figures and loss of wealth through coronavirus, plus the question of when the latter would be measured.[60] Thirdly, there was the supervision of spending. Could the Commission do this alone or would the member states monitor it too, as The Hague advocated? The parallel talks on the seven-year budget were all about the total sum and the deductions for net contributors. In both cases the question arose as to whether payment could be conditional on respect for the rule of law (with everybody thinking of Hungary and Poland).

On the morning of Friday 17 July, summit chair Michel received the 27 government leaders and the Commission president in Brussels. The first day passed calmly but from the Saturday onwards irritation crept in. While the big four (Merkel, Macron, Conte, Sanchez) swore they would not agree to less than €400 billion in grants, Rutte & Co. refused for two days and nights to go above €150 billion.[61] That chasm had to be bridged. In the night of Sunday to Monday, Charles Michel linked the two big dossiers together. "What if we make it 390 billion in grants, just under the 400?" he proposed. With €360 billion in loans, the total coronavirus fund would amount to €750 billion. Regarding the budget, the frugal opposition was placated with a reduction in the total sum, to €1,074 billion, and an increase in their rebates.* Several innovations were abandoned too, with cuts made to the extra money for healthcare, for example. Supervision of spending of the Covid money was set up in a rules-politics balancing act, whereby the Commission was made responsible, while the member states were given an "emergency brake". The rule of law disappeared from the table, transferred to the Council of Ministers and the Parliament. Nobody now felt like confronting the china shop with that elephant.[62] After four days and nights of negotiation, a jubilant Michel sent out a message in the early hours of Tuesday 21 July: deal!

"Relieved", was how Angela Merkel described herself when it was over. With the recovery fund we "have agreed on a response to the gravest crisis in the history of the European Union", she said.[63] As she had on 18 May, she gave a press conference along with Macron, side by side this time. The French president spoke of an "historic agreement" and stressed what was new about it: the Union could take on debt and more than half the recovery fund consisted of grants. He repressed an all too radiant sense of triumph. After all, the German chancellor next to him kept stressing the exceptionality of the pandemic state of emergency, the singularity of the gesture. But the

---

* The latter to the annoyance of both Commission and Parliament, which would have liked to do away with this infringement of the equality principle once wrested from them by the obstinate Margaret Thatcher.

Frenchman knew that anyone who crosses a bridge once will cross it again. A precedent had been set.

"An historic moment for Europe and for Italy", Prime Minister Conte celebrated, and his Spanish colleague Sanchez echoed his sentiment. The Portuguese Costa, in March still the mouthpiece of Southern anger, put a photo of himself on Twitter wearing a huge smile. Rutte and Kurz, less euphoric, spoke of "a good result".[64]

The next day commentators underlined the innovative nature of the debt issue. A market was emerging for EU debt securities, which might grow with time. "Brussels" had got itself a credit bank. Without using the inflated language of some commentators ("Hamiltonian moment"), something essential seemed to have changed. Confidence in Europe was increasing, the value of the euro rose against the dollar. How enough revenues would be generated to pay back the debt over 30 years was left an open question by the leaders.[65] You cannot decide everything in one go. Despite this uncertainty, the credit rating agencies – in the previous crisis the tormentors of the peripheral eurozone countries – gave the new debt securities the coveted triple-A status. From India the Dalai Lama declared on behalf of the voices of conscience that it was "heartening".[66]

A few days after the agreement, a tired Ursula von der Leyen looked back in the company of a handful of European newspapers. Just once she faltered, when the distressing start of the Covid crisis came up – the face masks, the closed borders, the bitter quarrels over money – and asked her spokesperson, "'*In den Abgrund schauen*' (staring into the abyss) – how do you say that in English?"[67]

Act II

In late 2020 the pandemonium became the backdrop to a relentless battle over the lifesaving vaccine, fought out under the bright lights of the main stage of world politics. The hellish, corporeal panic of the spring had been allayed in Europe. With the first vaccines the end of the ordeal seemed in sight, although new waves of infection and virus variants demonstrated that the road back to normality would be a long one. Fractiousness and impatience had taken the place of fear and panic.

The conflicting emotions were represented at the European summit of December 2020. Blockage by Hungary and Poland was avoided. The July agreement in principle on a coronavirus reconstruction fund was made definitive. All hope lay with deliverance by vaccination. The imperilled citizens pressed around the stage, restlessly watching the battle over vaccines surge back and forth between propaganda and healthcare, between dynamism and foot-dragging.

THE VACCINE WARS
(3 MARCH 2020–9 MAY 2021)

In the worldwide battle for vaccines and personal protective equipment, the European Union experienced how hard power and the capacity to act trump agreed rules and price incentives.

In his classic 1919 work on the wartime economy, philosopher and economist Otto Neurath wrote, "War forces a nation to pay more attention to the amount of goods which are at its disposal, less to the available amounts of money than it usually does".[68]

This lesson was in place for subsequent phases of the pandemic, in which the main players were judged on their ability to protect their populations. It took shape first of all in the question of access to a vaccine, which was a matter of prestige, as the British government realized. It all too readily attributed its effectiveness as one of the world's fastest at inoculation (a 90-year-old Englishwoman received the first injection on 8 December 2020) to Brexit liberation from the Brussels regulatory straitjacket.* That was not all. Any state that vaccinated its citizens quickly would be getting its economy up and running again, instead of languishing in successful or partially successful lockdowns.

The American government very quickly sensed that this was a war. In early March 2020 it emerged that Washington was bidding a great deal of money for the German company CureVac, with a proviso that it produced its anticipated Covid vaccine exclusively for the US. Economics minister Altmaier reacted fiercely: "Germany is not for sale".[69] An SPD parliamentarian spoke of an "extremely unfriendly act". In response the German government took a large share in the company, as protection against foreign takeovers. That indicated a move towards medical geopolitics. But Berlin did not prevent another German company, BioNTech, from entering

---

* Despite its Brexit claims, this British capability was founded upon EU regulations that remained in force in the UK until 31 December 2020. These permitted an accelerated procedure on condition that the member state concerned accepted responsibility for any failure, whereas after the full procedure, responsibility was placed on the manufacturer, a more cautious variant to which, tellingly, the EU member states gave preference.

into collaboration with the American pharmaceuticals giant Pfizer. By contrast the British government was busily encouraging Oxford researchers to sign up with a British-Swedish company, rather than an American one. France, too, which had acted robustly in the face-masks scrummage, collided head-on in the vaccine race with the laws of the war economy. The shock there came in May 2020, when a boss of Sanofi, the pharmaceuticals giant of which France is so proud, claimed that because of financial ties, a Covid-19 vaccine would go first to the US. President Macron, hopping mad, summoned the heads of the company to the Élysée.[70]

At the same time, the national governments saw that the Commission was not geared to dealing with forces of this kind. The masks procurement flop in February and March 2020, not even admitted to by von der Leyen, fed the scepticism as to whether she would succeed in securing a vaccine in a timely manner. Four member states preferred to keep the whole business in their own hands; Germany, France, Italy and the Netherlands joined forces. In early June 2020 their four health ministers signed a covenant on a "European alliance for a vaccine". Shortly afterwards they announced an agreement with Anglo-Swedish AstraZeneca for delivery of between 300 and 400 million doses, possibly from late 2020 onwards.[71]

A success, then, but reactions were mostly critical. Because out of the spring pandemonium of acute shortages and bitter division it was possible to draw quite different conclusions. A disruptive conflict of interest over medical supplies; a visible lack of solidarity at a moment of truth: few leaders wanted to live through that a second time. Commission president von der Leyen was very much put out by the timing. She was on the point of launching an "EU vaccine strategy" herself. Belgian health minister De Block called the quartet's initiative "unreasonable", saying it would "weaken everyone".[72] Other member states too complained about it being a "solo act" by the four, according to reports in the Dutch press, at which point The Hague pulled back.[73] Prime Minister Rutte assured everyone that the initiatives could be "slotted together". Synergy. Great.

This minor collision reveals a tension in European events-politics: the clout lies with the member states, legitimacy with the institutions. The four had given their initiative a proper European embedding, making it open to others, involving Brussels and promising that the doses would benefit "the European population", rather than giving precedence to their own citizens. Yet that did not suffice. The Commission's honour had been impugned and distrust generated in other member states.

Perhaps it is time for a more relaxed view of the interplay between governments and institutions, of what ten years ago the German chancellor christened the "Union method".

The political need for joint action, among government leaders as elsewhere, won out over doubts as to whether "Brussels" had what it took. The Commission was therefore allocated a crucial public health task. The decision to give it a mandate – one of the most far-reaching policy choices of the pandemic along with the creation of recovery funds – was taken relatively casually in June 2020. It was not widely discussed in parliaments or in public, in fact it is fairly hard to discover which body formally took the decision and when.[74]

What happened behind the scenes in vaccine negotiations between Brussels and pharmaceuticals companies from July to December led afterwards to countless reproaches, heated debates and quite possibly future parliamentary inquiries. What is clear is that, with a team composed of seven nationalities, the Commission led the negotiations. The team reported weekly to a steering committee made up of 27 officials, one per country. A fund of €2.7 billion was put together to support vaccine development. Member states were not allowed to compete against each other in the negotiations and the Commission took over contact with AstraZeneca from the vaccine quartet. On 31 July the Commission announced a success of its own: a deal with Sanofi for 300 million vaccine doses. Production would take place in Europe, specifically in Germany, France, Italy and Belgium.[75]

Weaknesses were evident nonetheless. Health commissioner Stella Kyriakides from Cyprus is considered a lightweight and her sluggish department has more experience with food labelling than with cut-and-thrust pharma deals. A top official from the Commission's tougher trade department was sent in to help out. Support from the member states was at a bureaucratic level. Politically the capitals were not on top of it all, and neither was the ambitious health minister Jens Spahn, representing Germany's presidency of the Council of the EU, who reported to colleagues several times that everything was going well.[76] In the Commission his compatriot von der Leyen relied on a very small staff. She too sent out reassuring signals. Several days after the British started vaccinating, with public impatience mounting, Chancellor Merkel reported at the summit of 11 December 2020 that all member states would receive the vaccine at the same time. She added relaxedly, "But whether the first inoculation will take place in all 27 member states at exactly the same time of day, whether the needle will go in at the same second, I don't know".[77]

The explosion came on 18 December when *Der Spiegel* spoke of a "planning disaster"; German and European citizens would run short of vaccine doses. The report was the opening salvo of an attack on the EU choice of policy. Had an offer of 500 million doses from Pfizer been turned down? Had Franco-German pharmaceutical rivalry played a part? Had the Commission pursued a low price to prove the "surplus value" of Union membership, or had frugal member states reined in EU spending?[78]

In Germany there was disbelief and exasperation that British, American and Canadian citizens were being given a vaccine – developed in Mainz – before German citizens. After political pressure on the European Medicines Agency, the first inoculations in the EU took place between Christmas and New Year. A reporter for *Bild Zeitung*, curious as to whether the agency, based in Amsterdam, was working "24/7" as promised, noted with fury that the lights in the building went out at 11.00 every evening and did not go on again before 7.00 the next morning. Rarely had pharmaceutical rules-politics been so mercilessly caught in the European public spotlight.

Why did vaccination in the EU happen so much more slowly than in the UK, in the US or in Israel, the country that in January 2021 grew to become the uncontested leader at getting shots into arms? There are two sides to the story: on the one hand the purchase of vaccines at an EU level and on the other the inoculation campaigns, the responsibility of national, regional and local governments. Much went wrong on both fronts. In this account acquisition is central, since in contrast to the distribution logistics it was made into a European *res publica*.

Speed of action was lacking. The vaccination campaign launched in the United States in May 2020 was given a name out of *Star Trek*: Warp Speed. The need to act quickly overrode many other considerations in Washington. In Europe, by contrast, haste came up against the opposing forces of rules-politics. Some were structural: circumspection, frugality, participation of all member states in the negotiations. Others had to do with the pandemic: vaccine scepticism, political powerlessness to assess medical risks, a latent aversion to the financial power of Big Pharma. Because of the latter, European governments refused to take over legal liability from the pharmaceuticals companies. Washington and London did so and won themselves three weeks, and many lives. London also focused its efforts on the first injection, even though the vaccine offered optimal protection only after the second. That gamble too was justifiable, given the high price of lockdown for the economy.

The EU failed to absorb the fact that lives are ultimately saved by things, not by contracts. When in private circles in Berlin an expert spoke of a pandemic "war economy", which required the mobilization of all available means, the rebuff was immediate: Germany has a market economy.[79] Whereas the EU concentrated on the purchase and development of a vaccine, the US operated across the full spectrum, spending its dollars on acquisition, research and production, not just on pharmaceuticals companies but on manufacturers of vials, hypodermic needles or bioreactors. Washington, mindful of the presidential slogan, opted for America First. In exchange for investment in pharma, the US authorities received the first 100 million vaccine doses produced in America. Consequently the Pfizer factories on American territory produced purely for the home market, whereas Pfizer factories on EU territory served both the Union and the rest of the world.*

Even the most powerful lever, money, was not mobilized optimally by Europe. The Brussels kitty of €2.7 billion stands in stark contrast to the $18 billion made available for vaccines by Washington in May 2020.[80] The Commission was keen to prove that as a bloc you are in a stronger negotiating position than you would be if member states were bidding against one another, or even snatching vaccines away from under each other's noses. For that reason, critics say, it was too avidly fixated on the price, at the expense of speed and security of supply. The institution has failed to refute that allegation. The British vaccine taskforce, a top team put together from the private sector by Boris Johnson in May 2020 – whose head Kate Bingham, a venture capitalist, became a national celebrity – had a very different approach. "We ended up with agreed prices per dose and an agreed schedule", Bingham said later. "But it was all about 'How do we get the vaccines quickly?' rather than 'Could we shave another 50p off each dose?'".[81]

Over the course of January 2021 tensions rose. France, Portugal and Spain announced they would have to pause or at least slow down their vaccination campaigns for lack of supply. The culprit was AstraZeneca, which reported on 22 January that until March it would be able to provide no more than a quarter of the agreed 100 million doses. Meanwhile the British-Swedish company was fulfilling its agreement with the UK. Von der Leyen jumped up and down, but boss Pascal

---

* Hence Pfizer delivered to Canada not from the nearby factory in Michigan but from Puurs in Belgium.

Soriot did not deliver. In Germany "vaccine nationalism" was now gaining ground. Opposition party AfD and representatives of coalition partner the SPD declared that Merkel and Spahn (both CDU) should never have farmed out the task to Brussels. Their job is to protect German citizens, so the argument ran, not European citizens.

Under this pressure, emergency measures were put on the table in Brussels. On 29 January the Commission stipulated that member states were permitted to impose an export ban on vaccines manufactured on their territories and could force companies to make their export plans public. At the request of the Commission, the Belgian authorities inspected an AstraZeneca factory to find out whether it had delivered vaccine doses to the UK. There were assiduous efforts to gain logistical control over vaccine movements. Frustration at the fact that millions of doses of the AstraZeneca vaccine produced in the EU were going to the UK while precisely none were coming in the opposite direction led to a blunder. In a fit of carelessness, without consultation, von der Leyen decided to invoke an emergency clause in the Northern Ireland protocol, one of the most sensitive agreements of the Brexit negotiations, that allowed the closure of the border between Northern Ireland (UK) and the Republic of Ireland (EU).

This was panic at play. Events-politics requires a sense of proportion and robust judgement. The benefits of closing an alleged surreptitious vaccine route in the Irish border area are as nothing compared to the reputational damage to the Union that resulted from this reckless move so soon after the British departure. During divorce talks with London the EU had hammered away time and again about the importance of respecting the Good Friday Agreement as a minimal guarantee of peace on the Irish front. Freedom of movement between Ireland and Northern Ireland was practically sacred, and it had forced the British, with their fervent desire for control of their own territory, to compromise. It was the hurdle at which Theresa May's government fell in 2019 and that her successor Boris Johnson had bluffed his way past by means of the Northern Ireland protocol. In von der Leyen's border strategy one crisis therefore collided with another, Brexit with the pandemic. The Taoiseach immediately called her and within hours the measure was withdrawn. But the harm had been done. Rapid rectification of the mistake did not extenuate the blunder; the memory of it remains.

In the run-up to the EU summit of March 2021, the British–European quarrel was resolved. Both sides recognized just in time that escalation would be highly destructive and put human lives at risk in the pandemic. Among themselves the government leaders discussed an export ban, pressed for by France, Germany and Italy in particular. Because of the interlinkage of production chains between the British Isles and continental Europe, the prime ministers of the Netherlands and Belgium advocated caution. Their countries are dependent on medical imports, while they also derive jobs from production and export. Yet they too acknowledged the unreasonable selfishness of British vaccine politics. Leaders from Central and Eastern Europe, realizing that, left to their own devices, their countries would have been at the back of the vaccine queue, declared themselves satisfied with the joint approach.[82] The general conclusion was that the Union would not simply close its borders, instead it would leave an export ban hanging over the market as the ultimate means of exerting pressure. It was a new sense of territoriality.

The logistical obstacles that vaccination campaigns in almost all member states came up against in the first few months of 2021 were only in part a result of the Brussels purchasing strategy. The contrast with Israel is telling. It headed the earliest vaccination lists by a large margin, with an inoculation percentage of more than 40 per cent in early February 2021. The next group of countries lagged far behind, led by the UK on 18 per cent and the US on 9 per cent, followed at a distance by Italy, Germany and France (roughly 3 per cent), with the Netherlands and Bulgaria trailing at the rear. Why was Israel, with its nine million inhabitants, so much quicker than comparably small and wealthy EU states? *The Economist* conceded it was logical that Israel would be better at waging war than Austria; it seemed harder to fathom why the same would apply to public health.[83]

But winning a war, as the Israelis know, is about more than tanks or drones. It turns on the ability to mobilize an entire economy, an entire society, for a single purpose. All other interests must be subordinated to that and there is no room for complaining or dawdling. Israel, at war since its birth in 1948, is world champion at mobilization and so it was able to run vaccination as a military operation. From EU sources the defence was heard that Israel had paid twice the price for vaccines and had promised to provide Pfizer and Moderna with patient data. There is a debate to be had about the latter, but the former? How much is a human life worth?

In April 2021 the vaccination campaigns in the EU began to pick up speed. Overall, more shots were delivered daily than in the UK or US. It seemed European countries would be able to open up their economies and social life with a delay of around two months. In the black ranking of excess deaths, by mid-

May 2021 the British and Americans were ahead of the French, the Germans and the average for the EU, although several individual member states (Belgium, Hungary) had done worse. When this phase of the pandemic is over, we will have to do the sums: how many infections, how many deaths, how many immunized, what worked and what didn't?

In the aftermath of the pandemonium the vaccine wars are now being fought out on various public stages. The medical battles at home are slowly being settled, it would seem, but the geostrategic battles rage on. Whereas China, Russia and the US see medical supplies in part as geopolitical levers, Merkel, Macron and von der Leyen started out together on the classic path of world health politics: the promise of help to everyone and universal access to a vaccine. After the mortifying spring weeks of 2020 in which their own populations were forced to watch as China and Russia – indeed even Venezuela and Cuba – came to the aid of Italy and Spain, by May 2020 the EU had resumed its favoured role of donor and benefactor (for example by donating billions to the Covax vaccination programme).

There is an unresolved tension between the Europe of world health politics, prepared to offer help beyond its borders, and the pandemic Europe that takes account of the primary task of protecting its own citizens. Can you be proud of vaccine exports when your own people are running short? The acute phase of this medical dilemma is over, but in global politics – as we shall see in Chapter 5 – the pandemic has made clear time and again how Europe struggles to do justice to its most cherished values while also protecting its own place, power and narrative on the world stage.

DISBURSEMENT UPROAR
(10 DECEMBER 2020–10 MAY 2021)

In Year One of the Pandemic, the final political fight within the EU was over the rule of law. During the summit in the summer, Budapest and Warsaw had refused to conform to the constitutional conditions laid down for the spending of money from the coronavirus recovery fund. In accordance with the customs of rules-politics, the government leaders passed the hot potato on to other EU institutions (such as the Court), as they have been doing ever since Viktor Orbán returned to power in 2010 – but this time in vain.

In the dynamics of the pandemic, the highest democratic values became the focus of debate for the first time. The European Parliament, which traditionally throws itself into the breach on this subject, felt supported by the public. Northern European voters who in the spring of 2020 hesitated to help the ravaged South were told, "Europe is not just about money, it is also about values". The discovery of Europe's geopolitical isolation, caught between the Chinese-American geomedical politics of divide and rule, made it all the more urgent to know and articulate what binds Europeans together, how its narrative goes about the uniqueness and unity of the 27. Thus the debate about the rule of law and democracy became ideologically loaded, almost a clash of non-negotiable values, such that any compromise meant betrayal.

Yet the leaders did reach a compromise in December 2020. The EU Court of Justice was given a role in assessing compliance with the rule of law, although it will probably not reach a definitive verdict on a case until 2023. That meant everyone could go home without losing face: the prime ministers of Hungary and Poland, with their threats of a veto, because they have won time and their countries will not be excluded from the coronavirus fund; the other leaders because the new instrument remains in place (the main concern of Western Europe) and the coronavirus recovery fund can make a start (the priority of the South). The urgent need to provide funds to those worst affected overrides the desire to curb autocratic tendencies within the Union immediately.

The conflict reveals a tension between Europe's democratic values and its geographic ambition, between faith in liberal democracy along nineteenth-century lines, as anchored in the Treaty, and an ambition realized step by step since 1989 to encompass the whole of the continent. The pandemic, the great revealer, makes it hard to paper over this conflict. Europe's founding dilemma looks oddly like that of the young United States between the Declaration of Independence in 1776 and the Civil War of 1861–65, which put an end to slavery in the southern states. As in the US, it may take two or three generations for the tension between founding principles and continental unity to be resolved (all the more so because the EU will not go to war, as President Lincoln did, to bring value-violating states into line).

This tension between fundamental democratic values and geopolitical aspirations is stronger in Germany than in any other member state. The postwar self-image of the Federal Republic is based on respect for civil rights. But overcoming Europe's East/West fault line – which divided Germany itself during the Cold War – is also a state religion, and German trade with the foursome Poland, Hungary, the Czech Republic and Slovakia is as great as with France. Whereas

Dutch prime minister Rutte could freely philosophize in the Dutch parliament in September 2020 about a European Union "without Poland and Hungary", and you could hear similar noises in Paris with regard to Schengen, in Berlin it is unthinkable.

So Angela Merkel, holding the rotating presidency of the Council and therefore leading the talks with Orbán and Morawiecki, banked on continental unity and put up with the blots on her liberal escutcheon. The German chancellor is the only "Western" European leader who commands the respect of both the Eastern troublemakers; her personal experiences under a communist dictatorship mark the way she deals with disagreeable circumstances. She deploys the political promise of a better future in a way that is almost old-fashioned, calling it "strategic patience". In her view the compromise over the rule of law is not a disavowal of European values but a means of keeping the hope of their fulfilment alive. If this Merkelian patience is truly to be "strategic", then in the meantime financial and political pressure must be maintained on the violators, or increased. The European leaders do not go nearly that far. Critical observers watch as old and new money from Brussels facilitates autocratic clientelism by the holders of power in Budapest and Warsaw.[84] The pandemonium has caused such practices to be played out in full view of the European public – an unexpected and welcome bonus. The democratic battle for law and justice is worth fighting in full view on the European stage.

Agreement on the mechanism for addressing breaches of the rule of law was not the only hurdle on the path to disbursement of the coronavirus recovery fund. All the national parliaments had to give their assent to the raising of the upper limit of the EU budget.* In Poland and Spain, for example, this forced governments to seek support from the opposition. Because of the deviation from monetary orthodoxy represented by the recovery fund (transfers, joint debt issue), much attention was paid to Germany, too. In the Bundestag and the Bundesrat majorities voted in favour, but opposition party AfD is taking a case to the Supreme Court, thereby blocking ratification. In a provisional verdict of April 2021, however, the judges in Karlsruhe decided that the recovery fund is not unconstitutional. Merkel's change of course has been maintained.

The greatest political tumult regarding the coronavirus fund arose in Italy. The badly hit country has a right to €209 billion of the €750 billion available. Much therefore depends on good use of the funding: Italy's economic growth and modernization, but also the very idea of a recovery fund within the Union. Does it create a precedent for debt sharing and financial centralization?

Former prime minister Matteo Renzi, the jealous leader of a left-wing splinter party, stabbed premier Giuseppe Conte in the back on 13 January 2021, Conte having developed during the pandemic from a colourless lawyer into the leader of a country in a time of crisis. It cost the second Conte government – a coalition between the Five Star Movement and the centre left – its majority. As grounds for the split, Renzi presented an opaque and far from ambitious recovery programme (which does not exclude personal and tactical considerations). President Sergio Mattarella was prompted to thank Conte

---

* For the period between now and 2058 the limit has been raised to 2.0 per cent of GDP.

and bring out the country's best horse from the stables, former ECB president Mario Draghi, to form a cabinet. The man
many see as having saved the euro in 2012 must now save Italy.

A cabinet of technocrats to calm a crisis? The Draghi government is made up almost entirely of politicians. If Mario
Draghi can be called a "technocrat" at all, then it is of an exceptional kind. In many respects he is a politician through and
through. Draghi is more seasoned and at least as clever as the
professorial Mario Monti, the former European commissioner
who at the height of the euro crisis (2011–13) led a cabinet of
technocrats in Rome after Silvio Berlusconi was driven out
by the leaders of the eurozone. Monti did the job of cutting
spending but did not convince Italian voters. On the European stage his clumsy manoeuvring lost him the confidence of
Merkel, which his country needed badly.

Draghi nevertheless speaks not just with the authority of
a technician who knows his stuff or has a plan but with personal, political authority. Take the famous Draghi promise of
2012 in London: the ECB would do "whatever it takes" to protect the euro against speculation. Those three words saved
the currency, the Italians believe, as do the markets. Draghi's
successor in Frankfurt, Christine Lagarde, discovered their
importance when fierce financial storms threatened as a result
of the coronavirus. As we saw in Act I of the pandemic, when
Lagarde casually said she did not feel bound by the standard
they had set, interest on Italian government debt promptly
rose. She came under fire from the presidential Palazzo Quir-
inale in Rome and the ECB had to put together an aid package
within a week.

The secret of those three words lies in what the speaker said
before and after them, brilliantly switching from technocrat

to politician. Immediately before, as an introduction to the ECB promise, Draghi said, "Within our mandate" (we will do whatever is necessary). In that "mandate" we hear the technician, shielding himself against difficult questions, brushing aside the notion that anything extraordinary is happening. But immediately after "whatever it takes" comes the trick. Draghi added, improvising in his Roman basso profundo, "And believe me, it will be enough". This bluff impressed the London speculators; apparently Super Mario still had instruments of financial torture in the basement. So it was that Draghi the politician deployed the personal authority he had gained over the years. With the ECB, and in consultation with Merkel and the government leaders, he tamed the crisis.

Mario Draghi showed his political stripes not just in the elite financial spheres of New York, London and Frankfurt but above all in his own city of Rome. As the top civil servant in the finance ministry (1991–2001) he worked with a succession of premiers and ministers, steering bills through parliament, skirting obstructions, motivating colleagues. Such powers of persuasion and pragmatic virtuosity are the political qualities that the primary processing of the economic consequences of the pandemic requires at this point. Just as the vaccine not only has to be purchased but shot into millions of arms before we can liberate ourselves from the lockdowns, so the manna of coronavirus funds not only has to be decided upon but spent if we are to escape the economic repercussions. The public all across the Union will look with Argus' eyes at the success or otherwise of European spending in Italy – partly in order to determine whether investment is sufficient to keep the Chinese out.

On 10 May, in the European Parliament, two European

commissioners, Italian former prime minister Paolo Gentiloni and Latvian former prime minister Valdis Dombrovskis, gave an update on the coronavirus recovery fund thus far. They expected that the first payments would be made in July 2021 and that the funds agreed upon in a state of emergency would form a precedent. "If this instrument works and we are able to agree on the new own resources to repay this common debt, I think we can have a serious discussion on further initiatives", said Gentilone, the voice from the South. "The more successful we are in the implementation, the more scope there will be for discussions on having a permanent instrument, probably of a similar nature", said Dombrovskis, the voice from the North.[85]

Aftershocks will undoubtedly follow, but in the year and a half since the virus arrived in Europe the main shock of the pandemic has been subdued. In essence the chronicle presented here makes two things clear.

First, the public health response fell short. True, all over the world and all over Europe the danger of the virus was underestimated. That reproach cannot be aimed at "Brussels" in particular. But when disaster struck the European institutions did not manage to speed up the role that fell to them and mobilize the resources needed; they spent far too long wading through a market economy after a war economy had dawned. They were acting in the wrong play. In future talks about strengthening the public health powers of Brussels this lesson must not be forgotten.

Second, the financial-economic response kept pace, the Union pulled off an unexpected feat. The lack of immediate European solidarity when Italy called for help will certainly remain in the memory, but within three months the principle of sizeable support for stricken economies was in place.

On behalf of her country the German chancellor crossed monetary red lines that were still sacred during the euro crisis, pulled the German public and hesitant Northern member states with her and rounded off 2020 by making an agreement with the resisting East – all in the name of the European public interest. In the rapid conversion of a public cry for help into joint action, the Union displayed an autonomous *vivere politico* and drew creative power from the hellish pandemonium. In Chapter 4 we will look more closely at this interplay between the European public and politics.

4

A public theatre

It is more and more public opinion that governs the people.
Alexis de Tocqueville,
Democracy in America[1]

Berlin, more than anywhere else, is powerfully aware that the public's ordeal in the pandemic can produce heaves and landslips, abrupt shifts and emotional eruptions in the European landscape, jeopardizing stability and mutual trust. It was this realization that led Angela Merkel to change course in May 2020 and lend special help to the countries affected.

Without the experience of the euro crisis, that decision would never have been contemplated. Old and new events interact and influence one another. Temporal sediments (to paraphrase Reinhart Koselleck once again) are constantly shifting. This demands of the politicians, who manoeuvre us through time, a seismographic sensitivity to aftershocks and displacements. The German chancellor noted how in the spring of 2020 harsh experiences from the previous decade surfaced. When €240 billion was made available in pandemic loans, Italy refused to accept the conditions – "our country is dying" said the leaders in Rome and Madrid – and so the money had to take the form of grants. Nor was it possible to ignore the fact that the Italian public's trust in the Union was plummeting and for two out of three Italians, leaving had become an option.[2]

Shifts in the public sphere are pure politics. The outcome is not just the sum of objectifiable forces (such as a country's trade balance, arsenal or technological capabilities) but also, indeed above all, a matter of humour and sentiment, gratitude and rancour, memory and expectation, words and stories, expressed in mostly unstable balances and changing majorities. Yet that is no reason to dismiss the public mood as fickle. It can be read, felt and influenced. Moreover, public opinion holds tremendous power within it, capable of pushing aside or shattering many supposedly objective realities. A fact that became visible during the pandemic; rarely before had the public been such a catalyst for big innovative decisions in the Union.

The Hague and other Northern capitals also read the coronavirus crisis as a sequel to the euro crisis, but in revealing contrast to the chancellor in Berlin, they saw it as a simple repeat, the same collision once more. So they missed or ignored three major changes in the public and political sphere. The first was the pandemic rhetoric. During the euro crisis a Northern story about responsibility and discipline collided with a Southern story about empathy and solidarity. There was something to be said for both, which led to agreements about "conditional support": more solidarity and more discipline too. In the pandemic, however, the harsh discipline story was inappropriate and no rhetorical match for the powerful solidarity narrative, especially since the public all over Europe felt menaced by the virus. The human suffering was too great, the responsibility argument inapplicable, as

Merkel realized. For the North – or what remained of it – this rhetorical weakness translated as strategic weakness.

Secondly, in previous years the German debate had already shifted among experts. Since the banking crisis, economists, intellectuals and politicians from the US, the UK, France and Italy have been questioning the German, "ordoliberal" perspective on the economy and the euro. A new generation of German economists, educated in part at American and British universities, does not swear by moral hazard alone and has now taken up posts in bureaucracy and journalism.[3] In geological terms, a steady trickle of words has worn, drop by drop, underground cavities and tunnels in the formerly solid German monetary doctrine. As a result, Merkel's agreement with Macron came up against less resistance from experts than it would have done ten years earlier. A landslide in German thinking.

Thirdly, the North was starting to experience the impact of Britain's departure from its seat at the European financial table. In matters of money, London was always the general leading attacks by the frugality troops, prepared to use its veto to torpedo any agreement it found too expensive – with reference to the grumbling, restless public at home.* Thus in the euro crisis London blocked the deployment of the Union budget for almost-bankrupt member states; in the pandemic, without Brexit, it would probably have done the same. The UK has never seen the Union as a community of destiny; the pain and plight of the other members was "not our business".

---

*   The Netherlands and Austria have a veto too, but in a major negotiation about money in which the players are compelled into a unanimous agreement – a kind of tug of war until all forces are in balance – it brings less weight to bear.

Without this brake, definitively released on 31 January 2020, amidst the pandemic the European *res publica* translates more quickly than ever from task into form, and from promise into practice.

To the metamorphosis that Europe has been experiencing for three decades – from a system geared to rules-politics to a political body that is also equipped to engage in events-politics – the coronavirus crisis gave acceleration and a new twist. We have come a long way from the depoliticized Brussels rule-making factory that, out of public view, knocked together a continental market. The Union is stepping onto a public stage; its actions and movements are becoming more visible. In the situations of drama and conflict that a union of states with a single currency and shared external borders inevitably experiences, fatal choices and divisive dilemmas can no longer be concealed behind technicalities and procedures. The public demands a plotline and a place for itself in the action, the players are stepping into the light, a European public realm is taking shape.

Not everything is changing at once. Even today, depoliticization, the strategy of the old Community, remains the guarantor of predictability, legal certainty and trust between member states. But today's Union is at the same time looking for ways to increase its reaction speed and its capacity to act, and being forced to recognize that this induces politicization, with visible choices and democratic responsibility. A tension between the two approaches resides in the law and functioning of the Union's institutions as well as in public expectations. Some are attached to stability and caution, others want Europe to capitalize decisively on change.

Nevertheless, movement is mainly in one direction. Every

crisis that touches upon the *res publica* sparks a visible political battle and demands a theatre in which it can be fought out. Situations of immense uncertainty require improvisation, free choices in the moment at hand. The greater the threat, the brighter the stage lights and the more urgent the public call for solidarity. This in turn requires players who, with an authoritative story, are not afraid of the limelight. Uncertain times increase public distrust of activities backstage, and opposition and dissenting voices walk into the theatre too, demanding a role.

All these phenomena in Europe's dramatic metamorphosis have emerged in sharp focus during the pandemic, for example in demands from the public wanting to know what went wrong in Brussels with the purchase of vaccines. The public health crisis that is overwhelming all member states and affecting all citizens personally enlarges the shared public realm.

Improvisation

The pandemic continues to cause unrest and uncertainty. The virus is new, its infectiousness, deadliness and mutability unfamiliar. Those in charge acknowledge this. "This situation is serious and open-ended", said Angela Merkel during the early weeks. "We have to take 100 per cent of decisions with 50 per cent knowledge", said Mark Rutte. Even Macron, although initially on the rhetorical warpath (*"Nous sommes en guerre"*, "We are at war") modestly went on to make a distinction between "what we know" and "what we don't know".[4]

What do you do when you find yourself in an emergency

and existing knowledge, practices and rules provide no help? You have to improvise. The word "improvise" can have a negative cast to it, suggesting guesswork and a lack of preparation, but also a positive, creative side, as in jazz or the debating chamber, where the best improviser is the hero of the hour. A person who prepares an "improvised meal" – certain ingredients not purchased, more diners than were expected – will not venture to say beforehand how it will turn out. This example makes clear that "improvisation" merits a negative connotation if you ought to have known better and have failed to prepare, ignoring experience. But if you are forced to act from a standing start, if an unpredictable challenge arises, then improvisation is not a failing but a special quality.

When the euro crisis hit in early 2010, no one knew what to do. The situation was without precedent. Fresh surprises came thick and fast. From the start there were armchair warriors who believed the solution was perfectly simple, if only this or that were done. But the crucial risk of "financial contagion"(!) – the passing on of a financial conflagration from one member state to another – was not foreseen by any of the experts. No protocol lay ready. There were no instruments for jointly tackling a crisis, in fact there was not even a toolkit. In Maastricht (1992) it had been solemnly decided that the monetary union required rules only, and concerted action would have to be superfluous. In this respect the crisis forced a reversal in thinking, which did not come instinctively.

Two and a half years of trial and error were required by the European leaders before they managed to calm the euro storm. When in the spring of 2010 Greece was on the verge of bankruptcy, other member states were, strictly speaking, forbidden to come to its aid. Yet the leaders did not want to risk the whole eurozone shattering to pieces because of a local problem. During a hectic May weekend a rescue package of €750 billion was put together. It was legal ad-libbing (a special purpose vehicle under Luxembourg private law) but all eurozone member states agreed to it, just minutes before the markets in Asia opened. The central bank acted too. Herman Van Rompuy, chair of the summits, said this was "building a lifeboat on the open sea". The successful spring intervention was nullified in the autumn, however, in a memorable deal by federal chancellor Angela Merkel and French president Nicolas Sarkozy. At the fashionable beach resort of Deauville, both claimed to have achieved what their countries wanted, but their performance insulted their partners and alarmed the markets, with a bail-out for Ireland as a consequence. It was a failed improvisation, a poorly prepared *Alleingang à deux*. Not until a year later did the leadership of the eurozone abandon the idea that budget deficits were the chief cause of the problems and allow room for the alternative of a "banking union", which was the key to quelling the crisis in the summer of 2012.

In this stream of events the Union gained a series of new experiences, which make it possible now to distinguish beforehand between a promising improvisation and an inevitable fiasco, in other domains as well. Just as a musical improvisation is never completely free – it would be random and we would not understand what we were hearing – a successful political improvisation must fulfil three conditions. First of all it must feature unity and shared responsibility. If several members of the group speak uninvited on behalf of all, or if they all talk at once, discord results. For a brief moment this may be acceptable, but if it continues the public will see and hear only chaos and cacophony. Secondly, "will to form" is required, in other words the determination to "dispose of the future as if it were the present", as Hannah Arendt once put it.[5] If that is not achieved, we see impotence, half-hearted decisions that fail to subdue opposing forces, and underwhelmed voters and markets.

The third precondition for successful improvisation is the avoidance of opportunistic caprice, or more positively put, the grafting of a decision onto the root melodies of historical stories and concepts that the public recognizes. In the euro crisis their role was performed by the concepts of solidarity and responsibility, or empathy and discipline. The Southern countries insisted on the solidarity of all with the whole, whereas for the Northern member states the priority lay with everyone's responsibility for healthy budgets and banks. A classic clash, with the threat of an impasse, a double "no". But in the final sequence the union managed to do both things at once. First the government leaders, at the summit of 28–29 June 2012, linked two political decisions together: central bank supervision by the ECB (in the name of responsibility) and the option of capital injections into insolvent banks by rescue funds (in the name of solidarity). It was a double "yes": more responsibility and more solidarity. Then in September 2012 Mario Draghi, with an unlimited programme of buying debt – for many the one remedy that tamed the crisis – brought into play a monetary magic potion. The central bank appointed itself a "lender of last resort" for the eurozone as a whole (solidarity) but with inbuilt conditionality for member states who resorted to it (responsibility). This dual decision – connecting with the root melodies and at the same time demonstrating unity and "will to form" – made it possible to calm the financial storm.

Why were solidarity and responsibility so important in those years? Why did so many of the political players – Merkel, Sarkozy, Hollande, Van Rompuy, Barroso, Draghi and Monti – keep taking rhetorical refuge in them? In a situation in which existing rules, treaties or academic insights fall short and there is an urgent need to act, a politician has to choose a starting point in order to convince the listeners. In Europe, the public has long been receptive to stories that invoke values and virtues, from Christian, humanist, classical or other sources. From these narrative layers the improvising politicians dug up the root melodies that they elaborated on, the themes to which their concrete decisions could be variations. Thus they avoided the impression of opportunism and arbitrariness, and were able to have the decisions accepted in parliaments and by public opinion as free and responsible choices.[6]

It is against this background that we need to judge the immediate action taken during the pandemic. That too was pure improvisation, both on domestic stages and on those shared by the Union. At the worst moments we saw disinformation, powerlessness and ineptitude, as in the face-mask and vaccine debacles. By contrast, at its best moments, as in the recovery fund agreement of July 2020, the Union displayed unity, authority and self-awareness. That play received good reviews from the public. At other moments the tension between the old instincts of rules-politics and the need to act decisively resulted in miscalculation and zigzagging, as in the overhasty Commission decision of late January 2021 to close the sensitive border with Northern Ireland to enforce a ban on vaccine exports.

Solidarity and res publica

In the spring of 2020 the pandemic triggered a groundswell of uncommonly powerful national sentiments. Day after day each society counted and blessed the sick and the dead, listened to declamations by kings, presidents or prime ministers, absorbed regular reports from the front, sang songs from balconies and applauded medical staff in the evenings. All of Europe created – and saw, recognized and reproduced – these new national rituals.

At the same time, the neighbours were closer than ever: their despair and their lockdown behaviour, their intensive-care policies and death rates, their open or closed borders. Pandemic empathy crosses borders but observing the neighbours also had its uses at home. The media assessed their own governments by comparing them with others. Whereas citizens usually measure the performance of the team in charge against that of its predecessors or the promises of the opposition, this crisis enabled them to compare policy at home with that of the country next door in real time. The public wanted to know why Germany was testing more aggressively than France, why more people were dying in Britain than in Austria, why the Czech Republic was banning travellers from China, why Belgium was introducing masks while the Netherlands was not.[7]

But in the Union it went beyond comparison alone. Because of the interdependence of currency, market and mobility, the public experienced the repercussions in their own lives of decisions by neighbours. What if Germany pumped billions into its own economy and Italy could not afford to do so? What if Sweden took a lax attitude to Covid and its neighbours kept their borders open? As John Dewey deduced, a public comes into being at the point when people see the consequences of an act or an event and organize themselves to monitor or oppose it. In the pandemic this was not confined to invisible abstractions or future risks; all citizens felt personally, and from the start, how urgently and powerfully the established order was being disrupted. The response was obviously a public matter. Some national publics were quick to say to their neighbours, this decision of yours is our business too. Conversely, several national leaders were immediately held to account by a broader, European public. It was in this unexpectedly lively exchange that a new public sphere took shape.

Something of this kind happened for the first time during the euro crisis. Ministers and government leaders discovered that they were acting not just on a national stage in front of their own voters but on the European stage as well, which emerged in and through events. As early as the spring of 2010, Angela Merkel felt the heat of Southern anger. Even actors in supporting roles could be haunted for years by words spoken in careless moments. It happened to Eurogroup chair Jeroen Dijsselbloem after he sneered at the South in a German newspaper (*"Schnapps und Frauen"*).[8] Clever players learnt to use the opportunities provided by public performance quickly and strategically. In an effort to alleviate the fate of the Greeks, Syriza prime minister Alexis Tsipras and his government appealed directly to the European public in 2015, over the heads of fellow government leaders. In the full light of day, mediagenic finance minister Yanis Varoufakis shrewdly toured Paris, Rome, London and Berlin straight after his appointment, to persuade his colleagues to show goodwill and relieve his country's debts. Given Greece's weak starting point, he endeavoured to topple the prevailing austerity story with a torrent of words, to change the rules of the game. In the role of opposition, the Greek duo demonstrated that conflicts of interest in the Union occur not only as country versus country but as "discourse" versus "discourse" – in the public sphere.

In a pandemic that threatened all citizens, a fierce war of words broke out. Again it was a clash of values, on the subject of financial solidarity. In March 2020 Dutch finance minister Wopke Hoekstra inadvertently set it off with an insensitive proposal for investigation by the Commission into the absence of financial buffers in Italy and Spain. It was an offhanded swipe in the hope of applause from the Dutch home audience, but boos and hisses rained down from the European gallery and he had to slink away. The inexperienced politician – at the time of the euro crisis Hoekstra was still a consultant – had misjudged and underestimated the nature, size and mood of his European audience. Furthermore, this painful misstep came at the very moment Southern Europe brought into play an old desire from the euro crisis, with a call for the issuing of joint debt. It did so first of all, classically, in the letter of 25 March from nine government leaders to summit chair Charles Michel, but far more effectively several days later by means of a full-page advertisement in the *Frankfurter Allgemeine Zeitung* intended to gain the support of the German public for "corona bonds". The Italian mayors and politicians who endorsed it asked the Germans in passing to reprimand the Netherlands, a country it dismissed as a tax haven. Premier Giuseppe Conte gave interviews on German television and to the Dutch newspaper *De Telegraaf* ("Our friendship remains but come on Mark, help us"). Another striking example of communication with the public was by German ministers Scholz and Maas, who in early April placed an opinion piece in *La Stampa, El País* and three other southern European papers with the message that they would not respond in the way they had to the previous crisis. "We don't need a troika, inspectors, and a reform programme for each country drawn up by the Commission. What we need is quick and targeted relief".[9] In late April, Dutch premier Mark Rutte, during a working visit, fell to talking with a refuse collector in The Hague who called out to him, "Please don't give that money to the Italians and Spaniards". Rutte stuck up a thumb and said, smiling, "No, no, I'll remember that". The film went viral, and within an hour (!) it was causing a furore in the Spanish and Italian media. "Just you wait until one of your dykes bursts and you vanish into the sea", was the retort aimed at the garbage man by an Italian on Facebook. In public communication, European voters keep themselves and others sharp.

It is sometimes claimed that there is no European public space because we do not all speak the same language. That is nonsense. Applause, goals and catcalls are universally understood. The audience is sometimes reduced to the "civil public", the gathered participants in a civilized debate as they have organized themselves in European societies since the early Enlightenment.[10] Although the importance of this public debating sphere is immense, a "professional deformation" may be at work here. The public that politicians deal with consists of more than just rational citizens who send letters to the newspapers and vote every so many years. The audience mutters and grumbles, weeps and claps, it protests and waves flags, has wishes and bears grudges, and above all it demands a role on the stage, however inarticulate. These movements have immediate or potential political significance, as also becomes clear in European events-politics.[11]

Angela Merkel is sensitive to the pandemic danger of acute emotional eruptions in the European public sphere, or a precipitation of rancour that will eventually prove disastrous. Other Berlin players discern these forces too, like the prominent CDU politician Norbert Röttgen. "The categorical 'no' to corona bonds is economically well argued but emotionally fatal", he tweeted on 6 April 2020. Whereas for him emotion could settle the argument with the South, the German public, in its Habermasian form, was also open to rational arguments from the opposing side. Thus the Covid crisis produced the unanticipated spectacle of a debate in the German public sphere for and against euro bonds (such that the arguments in favour, previously almost amounting to treason, became a shibboleth of right-mindedness). A plea by authoritative economists in favour of euro bonds published in the *Frankfurter Allgemeine Zeitung*, underwritten by a well-known German ordoliberal hardliner, also appeared in *Le Monde*, *El Mundo*, *The New Statesman* and the Dutch *Financieele Dagblad*.[12]

As a result of this public battle of ideas, the Federal Republic freed itself from a certain hypocrisy that accompanied its European leadership until recently. The political leadership frankly admitted that aid for the South was partly a matter of self-interest, of export markets and economic stability. This in striking contrast to the euro crisis, when Berlin mentioned only piecemeal that it was defending its own interests and preferred, out of a sense of moral and economic superiority, to depict the Greeks and other debtors as "sinners". Of course the Greek government had indeed spent too much, but Germany successfully concealed the fact that the billions in support made available to Athens also served to stabilize the German and European banking system, that the low exchange rate of the euro brought about by sharing it with Southern Europe had served the country's export model well for 20 years, and that money lent against interest would still have to be paid back. Something comparable, although more subtle, occurred during the migrant crisis. That the chancellor kept the borders open for refugees from Syria in the summer of 2015 was a noble gesture, for which she received applause from Europe and beyond. But in Paris and other capitals it did not pass unnoticed that a rapidly ageing Germany could make good use of qualified Syrian professionals. Those who in such situations play only the moral tune and obscure self-interest arouse annoyance and aversion and shut themselves off from dialogue. Now that Berlin is talking about both solidarity and self-interest, it is gaining credibility and powers of persuasion, not least with the European public.

This new openness represents a real caesura in euro-politics. The currency politicizes. The honest conversation about the European economy that is starting up bursts through the discretion and depoliticization of the monetary "clearing house" that Germany and France established in the 1970s for their currencies and exchange rates. For years the economic and political gains and losses were concealed within it, and when that became impossible they were hidden in the balances of the ECB. But ever since the euro crisis, this furtiveness – which hampers communication and feeds hypocrisy – has fuelled a crisis of trust between North and South. If technocratic secrecy once served to channel emotions, "it is now the source of the emotional caricatures that it has managed to keep in check for so long".[13] As regards market and currency, and their successes and failures, openness and honesty are the right path to take. This means more politics, more visibility. It will inevitably lead to pandemonium when economic conflicts of interest emerge onto the stage. After the easy-to-read levels of debt and budget against which the currency union judges its members, the more complex labour markets, tax regimes and retirement ages are now coming into public view.

So it is for democratic politics – and first of all government leaders – to take responsibility before parliaments and opinions for the changes of fortune of the *res publica*.

In the limelight

During the euro storm two players took the leading roles, Angela Merkel and Mario Draghi. Each found the words to subdue disruptive forces. "If the euro fails, Europe fails", Merkel said in May 2010 to the German and European publics. "Whatever it takes", Draghi promised in July 2012 in London to the markets. Thus the politician and the central banker provided their improvisations with powerful personal authority. He became Mr Euro, she Frau Europe. There was a need for something of the sort, because if improvidence ushers onto the stage an unknown problem out of nowhere, then direction by officials wielding rules, precedents, mandates and objective criteria falls short. The audience will call for players who intuit the situation; it will demand embodied words that steer the play onto the right track.

In the Covid crisis the political players initially found it difficult to address the European public as a whole. For government leaders it was all hands to the pump in their own countries. Every home audience had practical and rhetorical expectations that could not easily be translated. The voice of the French president, for example, barely reached beyond his own national borders, even though he was a man of the stage as a self-appointed Monsieur Europe. No powerful words emerged from the Union institutions, a reticence that is to some degree inherent in its competences: public health lacks a federal mouthpiece along the lines of the ECB. While on the national stage several virologists soon took their places as prompts of the political leadership (Christian Drosten in Germany, Jaap van Dissel in the Netherlands, Marc Van Ranst in Flanders), no European counterpart emerged. Hardly any citizens have ever heard of the EU agency for infectious diseases in Stockholm.

In those dramatic spring weeks of 2020, the Commission president, Ursula von der Leyen, did not opt for an independent role in the European drama.* Only when a new script arrived in Brussels did she rally, at least in the eyes of the Brussels audience, with her initiative of a coronavirus recovery fund, by means of which her institution acquired prestigious new tools (the right to take on debt and, in due course, to collect taxes). This far from inconsiderable expansion of bureaucratic power will not in itself, however, give her the role of Lady Europe; in the first year of the pandemic it is the quiet firmness of Frau Dr Merkel that makes the biggest impression.

Authority in events-politics in Europe lies above all with

---

* For the naive YouTube film in which she, humming the European anthem, washes her hands according to WHO instructions, von der Leyen received no applause. She would have done better to leave that role to Gloria "I will survive" Gaynor.

the assembled government leaders. The Union is not a state and therefore does not have one or several politicians at its head but instead a collective. In the European Council the 27 elected national leaders, along with the presidents of the Commission and the European Council, meet roughly once a month, and that is where the spotlight falls. The dramatic staging of the summits – in the past before the classic decors of castles or hunting lodges, currently in the office-palaces of Brussels – reinforces the image of power. The cast is crucial. Practically all Europeans know one or more of the members: the leader of their own country, usually those of France or Germany, sometimes a Brussels president and often the opinionated characters who challenge the club rules, like Viktor Orbán, Silvio Berlusconi or Margaret Thatcher. All are democratically elected and in direct contact with their publics at home as well as with the larger European audience.

The press identifies the summits as the "locus of power", a story machine. Clashing personalities, historic decisions, battles over power and money – things happen! Right from the start, meetings of the European Council have drawn more than a thousand journalists from all the member states and far beyond. Media pressure contributes directly to the dynamic. In front of dozens of cameras it is unbearable, perhaps impossible, for leaders to acknowledge impotence by saying, "We couldn't reach agreement". Ministers or commissioners can permit themselves to say, "No comment, we'll meet again next week", but the summit circus cannot. The press can stoke division, break reputations, undermine claims. Precisely because of this implacable power, it propels the circle of leaders towards more unity and decisiveness than individual members think themselves capable of beforehand.

It is precisely its ability to stage combined democratic exercises of will in the public glare that enables the European Council to act as the institution of highest authority in the Union. When a problem cannot be dealt with at lower levels, the boss takes charge: *Chefsache*. In a company the boss is the CEO, in Berlin the chancellor, in Brussels the European Council – bosses plural. As far as content is concerned, any issue can become a *Chefsache*; the specificity does not lie in the "what", it is a matter of "when", of urgency and sensitivity, the right moment to act. Sometimes the intervention comes at the end of a decision-making process, if a difficult decision is required. Sometimes it comes at the start, if strategic direction needs to be given, new territories explored. Another typical *Chefsache* moment is a crisis, when the worst comes to the worst. Since 2008 the government leaders have needed to fill this storm-tamer role several times, quite often with great reluctance. Only the members of the European Council command individually and collectively the authority to mobilize the entire diplomatic and bureaucratic apparatus of the capitals and Brussels for a single purpose, and to take decisions that go outside established frameworks. For the Union this subduing function is vital,* as we are witnessing again in the pandemic.

The coronavirus became a *Chefsache* on Tuesday 10 March 2020. The previous Friday the European health ministers had quarrelled openly about face masks and on Monday 9 March Covid panic broke out on the financial markets. In consultation with the French president, the president of the European

---

* This essential role cannot be seen in the texts. The Treaty limits itself laconically to "When the situation so requires, the President shall convene a special meeting of the European Council" (Art. 15, para 3, TEU).

Council Charles Michel decided right away to convene a video summit the following day, the first ever. There was little preparation for the gathering and it felt awkward, both on and behind the screen. The seriousness of the situation was brought home to all the leaders by testimony from colleagues and earnest words from the Bank president, who also dialled in. Afterwards they realized a response would need to go beyond the scope of information websites. Joint action was urgently needed. Within a fortnight two more video conferences took place, on 17 and 26 March, followed by a fourth on 23 April; by then it was the lockdowns rather than the urgency that made physical meetings impossible. This frequency – the Union treaty foresees four formal summits a year – was unprecedented, demonstrating the immense pandemic uncertainty of those weeks.

"Zoom diplomacy" creates a dynamic of its own. Gone were the physical greeting rituals and the Brussels decor. In their place came 30 different office interiors, on a screen which on the first occasion read "Please, mute your microphone". As a background most leaders opted for the national and European flags; only Hungarian premier Orbán appeared without the blue-with-yellow-stars. Luxembourger Xavier Bettel turned out to have decorated his office with a pop-art Pringles painting from his private collection. Some leaders proved surprisingly eloquent on video. In the European Council you normally lose authority if you read something out – you are expected to be able to improvise – but several of the participants seized the digital opportunity to use an invisible teleprompter. In these circumstances the European Council, in the bad-tempered gathering of 26 March, managed to shake things up and share out tasks in the Union. The leaders gave the finance ministers a deadline for an agreement on pandemic credit and mandated the Commission to lay out an exit strategy, in collaboration with the summit chair – a route out of the lockdowns and towards economic recovery.

The physical distance was mainly an obstacle, however. It is virtually impossible to negotiate on screen. With four or five people it might just work, but not with 30. The bodily contact of handshakes, looking each other in the eye or feeling the atmosphere was gone; even though some virtual platforms provide "break-out rooms", these cannot make up for the absence of doorways, corridors or backstage spaces for a tête-à-tête. The European Council is pre-eminently a private and intimate gathering, with the mutual respect typical of an exclusive club – leaders only. No outsiders are allowed in, apart from a handful of EU civil servants, in stark contrast to the normal Brussels councils of ministers, to which each minister brings five advisers and where up to 150 people may be present. With so many eyes in their backs, no one takes a single step. In video conferences you cannot be certain of privacy: who might be watching or listening? Shortly after the meeting of 26 March 2020 a word-by-word account of the arguments was published in *El Pais*.[14]

Behind their screens leaders do not experience the physical round table that brings them together and so makes their unity tangible. Nor do they feel the pressure of the assembled European press outside the door. The interplay between invisible and visible spaces that is so productive for power never gets underway. As a consequence, the Union's video summits did not provide the supreme authority required by the state of emergency in the spring of 2020. Conversely, the successful physical summit of 17–21 July demonstrated how essential physical meeting is in calming a crisis. It was no accident that the meeting became the longest leaders' summit in 20 years. There was quite some catching up to do. Two months after the pioneering agreement between the German and French members of the European Council, the combined operational power of the 27 could be restored only at leader level.[15]

Embodying the symbolic entity visibly remained too much to ask, however, even when physical summits were occasionally possible again from the summer of 2020. There are times when the public wants to know what "Europe" thinks about something – not just one or other national capital or the inner world of Brussels but the Union as a whole. Who steps forward to speak when refugees drown off our coasts? Who offers condolences after an earthquake or during a pandemic? European words are needed, for the public at home and for the outside world. For non-European leaders a summit is a place, to recall the classic Kissinger Question, to get everyone "on the phone" at once. With that in mind, Chancellor Merkel invited Chinese president Xi to Leipzig in September 2020 for a meeting with all her EU colleagues. The European Council, as a kind of collective head of state, would give external shape to the entity. Because of the pandemic, that summit, intended as the highpoint of the German Council presidency, was ditched. What remained was a video conference for a trio of Union representatives – Michel and von der Leyen in Brussels, rotating Council president Merkel in Berlin – with their Chinese colleague Xi in Beijing. The operational unity was safeguarded (Michel and Merkel consulted with the other leaders beforehand) but the symbolic unity fell away. The meeting had no theatre; it took place away from the limelight and away from the eyes of the public.

Backstage

Having politicians in plain sight does not always satiate the public. When the drama accelerates and the performance becomes less certain, the audience can tell that they are not party to the whole script, there are things going on backstage: secret deals, private chats, powerplay. In crisis politics, therefore, democratic distrust can easily kick off. The public goes up to the stage, points out to the players that the storyline has changed and demands influence over how the play develops. Given that the Union was not designed for decisive action and rapid decision-making, this confrontation creates a new dynamic.

Strengthen the capacity to act: that is the first necessity the Union becomes aware of during and after every shock. With rules alone you can never bring disruptive forces to heel. Sometimes a brief effort is enough, but almost always new executive structures emerge from emergency measures. In the euro crisis, rescue funds were set up to offer billions in support, provisional at first and later neatly embedded in the Treaty. A resolution mechanism arose too, not to regulate all banks but to make it possible to deal forcefully with one bank, right now. In the migrant crisis the discreet border agency Frontex was converted into a robust Border and Coastguard Agency, with additional clout and more staff. Likewise, in the pandemic we saw the need to acquire stocks of medical supplies and to join forces for the development and purchase of a vaccine. After more than six months of borderless chaos, the European Centre for Disease Prevention and Control in Stockholm succeeded in drawing up a coordinated map, with regional colour codes, for the whole of the Union. It will surely not stop at this initial reinforcement of executive health structures. The Commission is launching new plans, and a conference on the future of Europe, to be concluded in 2022, will examine the matter.

Such backstage deployment of executive power is at odds with the public call for accountability and transparency. In the euro crisis this became clear with the infamous Troika. In a situation in which Greece, Ireland and Portugal received, from 2010 onwards, conditional support packages, the official triumvirate that spoke on behalf of a trio of creditors (Commission, Central Bank, IMF) had far-reaching powers. Experts at the level of department head came to tell elected ministers in detail how to cut pensions, or to specify which costs of which medicines must be refunded. The blatant discrepancy between the power of officials and bankers from Brussels, Frankfurt and Washington on the one hand, and decisions that to Greek, Irish and Portuguese voters felt like political interference on the other, ultimately led to fierce criticism of the Troika by the entire European public, which damaged the Union as a whole. Only after years of public indignation at this administrative arrogance, approved by the finance ministers in the Eurogroup, did a realization dawn within the Commission that at the very least people with political authority and accountability to the European Parliament must be sent to Athens, Dublin or Lisbon.

Strengthen the speed and resolve of decision-making: that is the second imperative of crisis-politics that the Union experiences each time another emergency arises. On that front too, deployment of executive power has taken place. See the permanent presidents, who forge consensus among the 27 leaders or ministers and embody EU decisions for the media and public. There are now presidents of the European Council (since 2009), the Foreign Affairs Council (2009) and the Euro-group (2005), far from coincidentally three circles that focus on decision-making, while for the legislative Councils the presiding chair continues to rotate on a six-monthly basis. Or take the step-by-step formalization of the "Eurosummit" since President Sarkozy first broke through the German "no" to the holding of meetings of eurozone leaders during the banking crisis. Herman Van Rompuy built on that precedent during the euro crisis, until the summit in 2011 was recognized and formalized by all member states as an institution. At a lower level, during the 2015 migration crisis the Integrated Political Crisis Response mechanism came into being, to speed up the sharing of information and preparation of decisions by ministers or government leaders. In the Covid crisis this body was deployed afresh.

During crises informal consultation groups often emerge, when formal structures prove inadequate. In the euro crisis one such backstage group became known to the public after carelessness with regard to protocol, namely the "Frankfurt Group", consisting of Sarkozy, Merkel, Brussels presidents Van Rompuy and Barroso, and bank governor Draghi. After their first, ad hoc meeting behind the scenes at the Opera in Frankfurt, where the departure of Draghi's predecessor was being marked on 19 October 2011, the group led the eurozone through the storm for six months like a kind of core cabinet.

Public suspicion is easily aroused. A body like the Frankfurt Group has no formal right to exist. For the public of smaller, unrepresented member states it is demeaning. A Director-ate of Great Powers – as at the Congress of Vienna in 1815 – is their primal fear. The press conference by Merkel and Macron in May 2020 about the German–French agreement on a coronavirus fund came as a blow to The Hague and Vienna. The presence of EU representatives who speak on behalf of the absentees tempers the affront. For their own and the general interest, inner circles would do well to present an agreement as a preparatory step towards a joint decision, not as a diktat, and to organize the public visibility of their meeting on a side stage that has a clear relationship with the main stage. During the pandemic too, backstage communication was unavoidable. An informal circle of leaders – Merkel, Macron, Conte, Sanchez, Rutte, Michel and von der Leyen – formed the "Washington Group" (so-called because of several IMF consultations in the same constellation by the finance ministers). Set up as a mission of reconciliation after the quarrels in March, this too came together at one stage in the margins of the July summit. We have likewise seen how the June 2020 attempt of four bigger member states to join forces for vaccine procurement in an "open alliance" was received badly by smaller member states, notwithstanding the vaccine quartet's reassuring noises about inclusiveness.

Clearly public scrutiny does not end when EU institutions are given the capacity to act. The mandate given to von der Leyen and her Commission in June 2020 to purchase vaccines on behalf of the Union came at a price; high expectations can lead to public disappointment and mistrust, as became clear from the end of that year onwards. What did the contracts contain? Why was there such tough negotiation over the price and not the speed of delivery? In a life-and-death crisis, forces of media scrutiny were unleashed of a ferocity to which the Commission is not at all accustomed. All the same, the institution learnt by the experience and tried to ride the wave of public indignation; when it started to feel it had been tricked by the British manufacturer of the "Oxford vaccine", Astra-Zeneca, it decided to make the sales contracts public and so to call upon the audience as a witness.

Yet a lively and productive European public space does not require in the first instance more transparency but a better readability of the political game. The Union is not lacking in transparency for anyone with sufficient time or money. Hence the bustling mass of professionals, be they lobbyists, interest groups or NGOs, that swarms around the Brussels decision-making factory, once theoretically upgraded by the Commission to a "European public sphere".[16] In fact these professionals collectively form a "policy space", a semi-public playing field for experts.[17] But that is rather different from a public space in the true sense, the arena of move and countermove, of word and response, of public accountability and visible opposition.

No government meets with the doors open. The light must be shone exclusively on the public podium of accountability. Negotiating and sweating goes on in the wings and backstage, where masks or roles are exchanged, line-learning is checked and eloquence rehearsed, new words are written and tested out, fellow players are encouraged and snapped at. What appears on stage is the result of all that preparation.

The spotlight of transparency is merciless; it blinds more than it illuminates. Shining the spotlight behind the scenes limits agility. The decision-making machine flourishes in the unlit calm of backstage, the safe space of permanent exchange, where mutual trust is rehearsed, where you can test out an idea and go beyond the strictures of your mandate. Although theoreticians of legitimacy like to imagine otherwise, transparency is not a panacea for the public. Being able to see a

maze of rehearsed and unrehearsed players does not help anyone to determine where responsibility lies. So a more urgent
need is readability, insight into the story and casting of the
Union, knowledge of the rules of the game and the grammar
of the European political theatre – a task both for the commentators in the press gallery and for the actors on the main
stage. The latter must take responsibility in public, in front
of the audience, for their own roles, for choices made in often
tragic dilemmas. Public responsibility is the necessary point
of departure for opposition.

Dissenting voices

The fact that, for several decades in Brussels, there was no
identifiable Government, and a taboo on asking for one, has
meant that no organized Opposition could take shape either.
For rulers the absence of an opposition – the people who make
your life a misery, thwart your plans and try to oust you from
office as soon as possible – might sound attractive, but for a
political system as a whole it is disastrous. If the voice of oppo-
sitional forces is not embodied, and if the call for such a body
is ignored, then the political arena soon becomes stifling.

Opposition has vital functions. It creates equilibrium by
reinforcing the "checks and balances" of a system and by pre-
venting abuse of power. As a mouthpiece for public unease
or unrest it guarantees vigilance and keeps rulers and the
public alert. If the opposition can show with its own plans,
legislative proposals or visions of the future that different
political choices are available, then the system will work
optimally.

Despite, or because of, the Brussels strategy of depoliticization, counterforces developed, first incidental, later permanent. In the years of turbulent crisis-politics, European
squares filled with demonstrators for and against the euro, for
and against border razor wire. Voters used their national ballot boxes to attack the European performance of their leaders.
Masks of technocratic obfuscation were torn off. Parties on the
flanks challenged Union membership.[18]

Nowhere did it become more obvious than in the United
Kingdom that the lack of room for involvement and alternatives within the Union could provoke revolt or departure. To
use terms drawn from political science, the lack of classical
opposition, or the familiar mode in which parties engage in
opposition to policy but acknowledge the system itself, gives
oxygen to opposition of principle, in other words to forces that
cast doubt not just on the government and its policies but on
the legitimacy of the political order as a whole.[19] The British
Leave campaign was certainly based on lies and false promises,
yet it is striking that it managed to mobilize an aversion to the
democratic impalpability of EU decisions. Decades of distrust
of Brussels rules-mania, impersonal decision-making and
policy choices placed outside the reach of Westminster were
expressed in the slick slogan "Take Back Control". "I think the
people in this country have had enough of experts from organ-
isations with acronyms", said Brexit front man Michael Gove
– a line like a dagger-thrust and a direct attack on the depoliticization machine.

We have already seen how Greek prime minister Tsipras
and his finance minister Varoufakis filled an important role
during the erupting euro crisis of 2015 by breaking through the
intangibility and lack of alternatives of the Brussels script. In

contrast to the Brexiteers, they made the political choices and dilemmas visible before the eyes of a huge audience, drawn from a broad public that was tremendously eager to hear their story. Premier Viktor Orbán did something similar in the refugee crisis, which stormed into the headlines at around the same time. The Hungarian likewise had no hesitation in articulating a coherent alternative to the line set out by the Union, in this case as a response to Merkel's *Willkommenskultur*, or culture of welcome. Against biblical charity he cunningly put up the Christian knight as a warrior for the Occident. This dissident too, an autocratic nationalist, sought public support on the opponent's terrain, especially in Germany.* On both occasions a brand new, unforeseen dynamic arose between Union-wide forces of government and opposition.

In the pandemic this development had a striking sequel. During the debate on the coronavirus recovery funds, the "frugal opposition" stepped onto the stage, a performance by Rutte & Kurz. In the medical state of emergency in which the Union found itself, their plea for less lost out to the call for solidarity. Neither prime minister was accustomed to the opposition role, since both were used to minding the pennies in European financial matters alongside financial custodian Merkel. Yet these opponents too attempted to persuade the European public. In the Italian daily *Corriere della Sera*, Mark Rutte stressed the extent to which insisting on strict

---

* Particularly memorable was Orbán's visit on 23 September 2015 to the Bavarian CSU leader Seehofer, who was at the time no less critical than his guest of Merkel's open border policy and who, despite being the leader of a party in the governing coalition, wanted to register his opposition on the point. Ebullient anti-Merkel demonstrators received the Hungarian as a defender of European culture – a Koselleckian tremor in the German underground.

supervision was not a miserly reflex but would enhance economic resilience and thus benefit the populations affected. Their arguments found a willing ear even outside the frugal countries, especially in liberal and conservative circles. In the German media, voluble German speaker Sebastian Kurz was a regular guest. Rutte was more reticent, but it was striking that FDP leader Christian Lindner quoted his liberal colleague in the Bundestag and in interviews. It seems that behind the scenes the Dutchman was mobilizing transnational networks of opposition and counterpressure.

Yet in this public health crisis no full, eloquent development of European opposition occurred. That was because of the specific nature of the emergency. Covid calls for experts. At the start of the outbreak there was a strong temptation to make virologists and epidemiologists partially responsible for restrictive measures. Scientists suddenly found themselves in the wings, acting as prompts. Several were even hoisted centre-stage. In that context, dissent is off limits. Certainly, public and politicians went on to discover that science does not speak with one voice but raises doubts by definition, generating its own opposition, so from time to time calls could be heard for coronavirus decisions, although of course informed by experts, to be more clearly embodied and assumed by political leaders. But by then it was already too late. The space for classical opposition to the content of decisions had been lost and the audience had once again flocked to alternative platforms.

The storming of the Reichstag in Berlin by around a hundred neo-Nazis and antivaxxers in August 2020 drew attention all over Europe. The face mask, a tangible restriction on bodily freedom, was a bone of contention for the self-appointed freedom fighters in Northern and Western Europe, whereas in traumatized Italy the mood had turned against mask-sceptics, such as national populist Matteo Salvini. Public opposition was supported by local or regional governors in situations in which the coronavirus rules were delegated to them. In the southern city of Marseille, local politicians voiced opposition from a group of shopkeepers and bar owners to measures from Paris. In London, dissident Conservatives canvassed support for an amendment that would give the British parliament a veto on every tightening of restrictions. Everywhere a battle broke out between compliance fatigue and civic duty, work and health, self-determination and solidarity.

While on national stages conflicts raged between sick bodies and working bodies – in which the odds changed continually, depending on death figures, job losses and vaccine promises – the European stage remained devoid of this dramatic dilemma. Our Union, the recovery funds said, is there mainly for the working bodies. Illustrative of the distance between the pan-European public realm and the theme of public health was the resignation of Irish European Commissioner Phil Hogan after he attended a rule-breaking fundraising dinner in Dublin. It was only after pressure from Irish public opinion and the Irish political leadership that he agreed to go. No pressure at all came from the European public sphere. The botched vaccine roll-out of early 2021 did turn the spotlights on the EU institutions' weak public health performance, but so far without a day of political reckoning.

In one state on the European continent the opposition originated from a contrary impulse – as resistance not to an epidemiological excess but to a nonchalance about combatting Covid: Belarus. In the summer of 2020 the world's first coronavirus revolt broke out there. From the start, strongman Lukashenko, 26 years in power, denied the existence of the pandemic. He diagnosed it as a "psychosis" and manfully recommended remedies such as vodka, saunas and tractor driving – a populist strongman infusion along the same lines as the praying Jaïr Bolsonaro's "a little 'flu", or Donald Trump's bleach injections. There was no lockdown. The Belarussian soccer competition went ahead, the only one in Europe, as did the 9 May parade in Minsk. Meanwhile many Belarussians became infected with coronavirus. On 9 August 2020, millions of voters used the ballot box to say the president should go, and tens of thousands took to the streets in response to the blatant falsification of the result. There were multiple reasons for the anger directed at Lukashenko, ranging from pensions to education, but the pandemic was the trigger for the mobilization of public protest.[20] Having failed as protector of the people, the president lost his authority and only violence was left to him. A trip to Moscow resulted. While the leader of the opposition went into exile in neighbouring Lithuania, Lukashenko diligently noted down the preconditions for help from the Kremlin.

This unexpected plot twist on Europe's eastern border is only one of the routes along which the virus, which took lives and brought society to a standstill, led in no time to tremors and tectonic shifts in geopolitics, presenting the European public with fresh questions.

A new beginning?

"Fellow citizens: our elites have failed us. It is time to create a European republic". Thus wrote an activist German-Italian duo in a manifesto published in *The Guardian* during the first wave of the pandemic.[21] According to the authors, after ten years of crisis the Union is definitively falling apart and a new Europe needs to be built from the ground up. After the example of the French citizenry that swore a Tennis Court Oath on 20 June 1789 – resulting in a revolution and the birth of the French Republic – the citizens of Europe must mobilize and anchor their constituent power. To use a term, again, from John Dewey, this high-profile minority feels like a "new public", obstructed by old forms.

Frustration at the slowness of Europe's political development is easy to understand, especially when a crisis hits. However, the capacity to anticipate, to get member states into line earlier for the sake of the common interest, requires a powerful narrative about the European *res publica*. As long as that story is weak, the public task cannot solidify into an institutional form and the Union will continue to respond to crises by improvising. This may be disappointing, but a revolutionary narrative will not break the vicious circle. The counter-forces of Europe's historical and constitutional plurality are strong, and the public is not receptive to the Promise of a new beginning.

There is movement all the same. The increase in awareness of European public affairs has been caused not just by the pandemic shock but by external forces that compel the Union to act and to have a narrative ready. On that great geopolitical stage, between the People's Republic of China and the United States of America, lies a vital new role for Europe.

5

Geopolitics: between China and the United States

How few Europeans understand how to smile; a couple of elderly French ministers, a couple of elderly Italian finance ministers, three English lords. Someone recently claimed he had never seen a German smile... But the Chinese people with their four-thousand-year-old culture receive splendid training in smiling. For it is neither more nor less than a discipline... Why after all make an angry or sad or disillusioned face? Why bare your soul in public?

Yvan Goll, *Die Eurokokke*

One feature of the usual script for plague: the disease invariably comes from somewhere else.

Susan Sontag, *Aids and its Metaphors*

Masks and bleach

On 6 February 2020 the Chinese president reported to his American colleague by phone on the coronavirus epidemic in his country. After a huge effort, it was now under control, said Xi Jinping, and China's economic growth would quickly resume. President Trump expressed admiration for the rapid building of emergency hospitals by Beijing and said he was ready to send experts and assistance.[1] A routine call.

Yet the implication of the conversation did not escape the American. The next morning he told a journalist, "This is deadly stuff, more deadly than your strenuous flu. You just breathe the air and that's how it's passed".[2] Whereas in European capitals at that moment only virologists saw orange warning lights flashing, in Washington news of the potential magnitude of the danger was quickly passed up to the highest political level. As early as the end of January – not one person had yet died of Covid-19 in the US – Trump was urgently warned by his top security adviser, "This will be the biggest national security threat you face in your presidency".[3] A week after his conversation with his imperial opponent – the economy was bowling along, the polls were favourable, the campaign coffers were filling – he was told by his campaign leader, "It's the only thing that could take down your presidency". To which Trump replied contemptuously, "This fucking virus – what does it have to do with me getting reelected?"[4]

In March 2020 the centre of gravity of the Covid pandemic shifted from China and South Korea to Europe. The next month it moved to North and South America, then back to the Asian continent, particularly India. On the world stage, everyone looked at everyone else. For governments it is useful to know whether a health danger is coming their way, to learn from approaches taken elsewhere and, if necessary, to offer or request help. But Covid-19 sharpens one dimension of such standard diplomatic traffic in an emergency: power politics. Unlike an earthquake or other classic natural disaster, a disease that is spread by human movement presents a great opportunity to put other players in a bad light, to weaken or manipulate them. Whose fault is it? Who is failing to get the thing under control? Who is helping? Who has a convincing story?

In the medical-political maelstrom of spring 2020, four insights, each of them revealing and at the same time perplexing, were attained by the beleaguered European public. First, in this disaster Europe was not going to be the world's Red Cross, but the pitiful victim. Second, in combating the pandemic the United States, the great ally that has taken the lead in all international crises since 1945, was absent, even abject. Third, it was the distant, strange and by most Europeans misunderstood or underestimated China that was able to fly in with tonnes of medical supplies. Fourth, to make the humiliation complete, the European public discovered that the dividing line between emergency aid and power politics is thin – and a benefactor can make demands. This series of experiences threw into disarray Europe's sense of its geography and history. On the world map of emotions, sympathy and respect swapped places. The pandemic forced Europe into a postcolonial view of the People's Republic of China, a post-Atlantic view of the United States of America, and a new definition of its own continental position and identity.

"Face-mask diplomacy" is the phenomenon that sums up the shifts most effectively. Italy, hit hard by the virus precisely because of the links between Lombardian industry and Chinese production centres such as Wuhan, was the first to be affected by the rescue efforts. On 12 March 2020, amid great media attention, a Chinese Red Cross plane arrived in Rome – not Milan, the centre of the epidemic, thereby underlining the diplomatic character of the mission. Foreign minister Luigi Di

Maio extolled the solidarity between the two countries. At the same time, the Italian government ordered medical equipment worth more than €200 million. Yet more flights with relief supplies followed, some from regional and local governments, and on three occasions they were accompanied by medical staff. Even some large Chinese businesses and organizations, such as the Jack Ma Foundation, came to Italy's aid. Nor were the dockland industries of Genoa and Trieste forgotten by their Chinese partners.

Serbia was another stop on the new silk road of sickness and health. In mid-March President Aleksandar Vučić came to the airport in Belgrade in person to receive a shipment of face masks. "European solidarity is a fairy tale for children", he said on that occasion. "I believe in my brother; I believe in Xi Jinping". In Prague, President Miloš Zeman made it known in late March that China was the only country to have helped the Czech Republic. This drove home the fact that ever since the 1950s the government in Beijing has had good knowledge of and strong links with many of the former communist "brother peoples" in Central and Eastern Europe.

It is a different matter for countries in Western and Southern Europe, which as an extension of Marshall Aid and NATO protection have enjoyed American support ever since the Second World War. Chinese face-mask diplomacy therefore raised eyebrows in the Netherlands. As a token of thanks for the aid that Schiphol Airport and KLM Airlines provided to China with discreet emergency flights in January and February,* three

---

* The last humanitarian flight from Schiphol to Wuhan took place on 7 February 2020 – at the time of the Xi–Trump phone call – when the virus was already circulating under the radar in the Netherlands but the authorities were still watching the Chinese assiduousness in amazement.

Chinese airlines donated medical supplies to KLM a month later. In April health minister van Rijn went to Schiphol in person to welcome a donation sent by Alibaba and Huawei. The Netherlands, never a beacon of diplomatic finesse, haughtily rejected as substandard a shipment of 600,000 masks it had purchased, an incident that the Chinese ambassador struggled to smooth over.

In the battle to look good, Europe put itself at a disadvantage. The tonnes of emergency supplies that had travelled in the opposite direction earlier in 2020, from Germany, France, Italy, the Netherlands and elsewhere, had been delivered without flag waving or drumbeats at the request of the Chinese. The country tolerates no loss of face. On 6 April the European Commission laid out the bare facts and figures in a press release – for the record, because for the theatre it was too late.[5] The leadership in Beijing was eager to shine its light on the full breadth of the stage.

To achieve that, all means were permitted. In Paris the Chinese ambassador hit out at French Covid failures so hard that his efforts rebounded.[6] Beijing does not yet command the subtle European codes of verbal exchange between the authorities and the public. In Berlin parliamentarians were shocked by a newspaper report that Chinese diplomats had urged the German government to put a positive spin on Xi's management of the crisis. The federal government told the Bundestag that it had declined to comply with the request. An alert commentator observed that not the foreign ministry but the interior ministry was responsible for such channels of communication. "What it signals is that China has become domestic politics for Germany. This points to the new reality of our relationship with China".[7]

The pandemic not only gave considerable scope to a self-conscious China, it revealed that China has a Europe policy that is not matched by any European China policy.[8] Public unease began to take shape.

The offensive Chinese response was set off even more starkly by a cynical display of American inaction. In the first ten months of 2020 more citizens, in absolute terms, died of the disease in the US than in any other country. Time and again the president played down the danger ("a kind of flu"), and paid little attention to experts and advisers. In late April, Trump recommended the use of disinfectant as a medicine against Covid. Hundreds of Americans ended up in hospital with symptoms of poisoning after seeking salvation in the cupboard under the sink.

Of course, the dark sides of the American dream do not come entirely as news to Europe: outbursts of racial violence, glaring social inequality, dispiriting interventionist wars, an opioid crisis, political polarization. Yet until the coronavirus pandemic, the brighter side dominated: democratic freedom, love of innovation, dynamism and faith in the future. Shortly after the disinfectant episode, an apposite piece appeared in the *Irish Times*: "Over more than two centuries, the United States has stirred a very wide range of feelings in the rest of the world: love and hatred, fear and hope, envy and contempt, awe and anger. But there is one emotion that has never been directed towards the US until now: pity".[9]

Domestic failure undermined America's claim to moral exceptionalism and global leadership. At the start of the pandemic President Trump was still behaving according to the familiar script. Referring to South Korea, he said, "They have a lot of people that are infected, we don't. All I say is, 'Be calm'...

The world is relying on us".[10] That was soon over, not just because in his own country the pandemic encouraged him to play America First in the worldwide battle for medicines to treat Covid-19 but also – and the two things were closely connected – because Trump subordinated every foreign policy performance to the question of coronavirus guilt and to rivalry with China.

American officials spread the contagious notion that the virus had escaped from a laboratory in Wuhan. Trump and his foreign minister Pompeo liked to speak of the "Wuhan virus", "Kung flu" or the "China virus", stoking up racist feelings against the Asian population across the world. When allies France, Germany, Italy, the UK, Canada and Japan rejected that qualification in a ministerial G7 video consultation in late March, the session ended in dispute. Washington then accused the World Health Organization of shielding Beijing and blocking investigations into the truth about the virus outbreak. In April Trump halted America's financial contributions to the WHO and in July he sent the organization a letter terminating its membership.

A rhetorical duel between two geopolitical adversaries filled the world's auditoriums. Pushed into a corner as the Superspreader of the virus, Beijing chided the Leader of the Infected World for its paltry Covid response. When America's State Department declared in late May that the Chinese government was "breaking its promise to the people of Hong Kong" with a new security law, the riposte by its Chinese counterpart on Twitter was a simple "I can't breathe", the final words of George Floyd, whose brutal death had stirred furious Black Lives Matter protests in all the States of the Union and beyond. American society became caught up in

double fight over bodies; in election year 2020, politics crept under the skin.

In this geopolitical battle of narratives, the Europeans were trapped. Both great powers were demanding to write their own version of the great coronavirus story. Xi Jinping wanted gratitude for the face masks provided; that meant not probing the Wuhan market or how the virus could have been stopped sooner. Donald Trump preferred not to hear about failures at home and demanded fidelity from his vassals, in a geopolitical conflict that was presented in Washington as a new Cold War between freedom and tyranny.[11]

A revealing incident shows how these forces made themselves felt as far away as backstage Brussels. The EU department for combatting disinformation (set up in response to Russian propaganda activities, it has since 2019 also investigated China) wrote in April 2020 in a preliminary version of a coronavirus report that Beijing was engaged in a "global disinformation campaign" to avoid carrying the can for the outbreak.[12] The text was leaked to the press, which led to fears that China would hit back by withholding medical supplies. After pressure on EU diplomats in Beijing, in which the word "repercussions" was used, the passage was watered down. According to the *New York Times*, an advisor to EU chief diplomat Josep Borrell intervened to postpone publication of the report. Criticism from the other side of the battlefield promptly followed. America's ambassador to the Netherlands, Pete Hoekstra, eagerly tweeted about Chinese intimidation, "Real friends don't do that".[13] In his response, in front of the European Parliament, Borrell described such fine-tuning as "the daily bread of diplomacy" and said his department never succumbed to pressure.[14]

Indeed, as Borrell observed, diplomatic work involves being, well, diplomatic. Drafts of difficult letters are often rather more cutting than the version the addressee gets to read. That does not necessarily mean you have sold your soul to the devil, merely that you have taken account of sensitivities, consequences, interests. Sticking firmly to principles in relation to the Chinese Communist Party may look valiant, but with too few face masks to protect your citizens you will soon start to feel short of breath.

So Europe drew its first conclusions from the dislocating experiences of the spring and summer of 2020. If it wanted to escape being squeezed between the People's Republic and the United States with their geo-medical divide-and-rule politics, then the Union would have to get its own production (or distribution) of medical and pharmaceutical supplies in order. Without strategic autonomy, no narrative sovereignty.

Against the desolate decor of the pandemic, on 3 November 2020 the American electorate chose Democrat comforter and healer Joe Biden over the Covid-denier who had held a superspreader gathering in the White House for his new supreme court judge six weeks before election day and become infected himself. It was a rather close call, a matter of mere tens of thousands of votes in the battleground states, contested and fought over in the courts and on the streets right up until inauguration day. Nevertheless, of all the plot twists the virus caused in the world, this was the most spectacular. Less than a year after its jump from animal to human, SARS-CoV-2 dragged POTUS off his horse.

In the great imperial duel, Europe's own metamorphosis became all the more urgent. Sticking to the text, as in rules

-politics, is not sufficient to see off assertive opponents and major global turbulence. This lesson from the foregoing decade of crises is true *a fortiori* on the political world stage. So with regard to both the People's Republic and the United States, the European Union would henceforth have to engage in events-politics, as a player with skin in the game, with power and a narrative. In respect of both, this was an historic turning point.

Colonized by China

Given the span of the Chinese concept of time, the face-mask diplomacy of 2020 no doubt felt like historical redress, an ironic reversal of the gunboat diplomacy of 1840–60, when first British and soon also French and American navy ships used violence to force their way into Chinese ports and markets – especially to sell opium. European drug dealers had now been replaced by the Chinese Red Cross. The looting of the imperial summer palace with which the expeditions culminated in 1860 is etched onto China's national memory.* Such colonial crimes marked the start of China's "century of humiliation" by the Europeans, the US and Japan, which in

---

* In case anyone should forget, black-and-white photos of smiling British and French soldiers sitting on the imperial throne have been allocated a place of honour in a permanent exhibition, opened in 2011, called "The Road to Rejuvenation" in China's National Museum on Tiananmen Square, where President Xi gave a programmatic speech a year later. After a British journalist travelling with the troops was tortured by the Chinese and died, the British burnt the summer palace to the ground. "What would *The Times* of London say of me", commander Lord Elgin is said to have remarked to a French colleague, "if I did not avenge its correspondent?"

the official history ended only in 1949, with the ascent to power of Mao and the Communist Party.

On the long march to the recovery of international authority, the People's Republic, despite its historical-cultural prestige and demographic weight, had to satisfy itself for a long time with a minor role. The Mao years brought China a position as the third great power, behind America and Russia, but also anarchy, violence and famine. Only as a result of Deng Xiaoping's economic liberalization was the country able to grow its way up out of poverty and backwardness from 1978 onwards, as the "workshop of the world". Even then, the arrangement retained many colonial features. Hardworking China made cheap goods for Western consumers and in return bought high-quality machinery and luxury items.

Over the past few decades, China's economic prosperity has been translated increasingly into political power. This first became obvious in 2008. On 8 August that year the world gathered in Beijing for the opening of the first Olympic Games in China, just a few hours after war broke out in the Caucasus between Russia and Georgia. The Chinese leadership used the opportunity provided by the sporting festival to deliver a clear geopolitical message: "We are back". Few European television viewers who watched the opening ceremony will have suspected how quickly this phenomenon would affect their own lives.

But the Olympic flame in Beijing had barely been extinguished before a major merchant bank in New York collapsed. In the light of a financial catastrophe following the Lehman bankruptcy, the American-European political and financial elite manifested so much panic and desperation that it forfeited a great deal of its prestige among voters and in the rest of the world. The debacle reinforced China's economic and political self-confidence, all the more so since it was the only major economy that continued to grow, soon overtaking Japan as the world's second largest. In November 2008 the G20 met for the first time, and everyone could see that the G8 of Western industrial powers had had its day. Global crisis consultations were pointless without China at the table and, in the process, India, Brazil, Saudi Arabia and Turkey were given a chair. The larger circle was unable to conceal the fact that in essence this was all about the financial relationship between the US and China. People began to talk of a G2.

In the wake of the banking crisis – and the euro crisis that followed it – many European governments found themselves in dire need of money, of investors, of buyers of sovereign debt, of export markets. China entered the picture as an economic mainstay. Along with the states of Eastern Europe and the Balkans, on Poland's initiative, Beijing set up the "16+1" forum in 2012, an annual gathering of regional leaders and the Chinese president.* It took shape as a series of separate conversations, true to the Chinese diplomatic tradition from imperial times of keeping relations with weaker neighbouring states one-on-one. Eastern European partners are interesting to China partly because of the Belt and Road initiative, launched by Xi in 2013, which makes Europe the western terminus of a New Silk Road. The railway from Belgrade to Budapest, partly financed by China, is a showpiece of these new overland routes.

---

* In 2019 Greece joined, as the first non-ex-communist state, while in May 2021, Lithuania announced its intention to leave; hence it has briefly been referred to as the "17+1"-forum.

The Chinese purchase of the Greek port of Piraeus – state company COSCO bought a majority share in 2016 after making investments from the autumn of 2008 onwards – has come to be regarded as a strategic failure by the EU as a whole. Because of the austerity politics of the euro crisis, Beijing was able to acquire a major geopolitical asset at a bargain price.* Chinese companies are also active in other Mediterranean harbours and on the Atlantic coast at places including Zeebrugge, Antwerp and Rotterdam, and Sines in Portugal. It is the maritime component of the Silk Road.

Yet Chinese expansion after 2008, from Athens and Genoa to Budapest and Warsaw, did not immediately throw the Western European public off its stride. After all, it was taking place among the weaker brothers of the European family. This changed as a result of a second shockwave, which started in 2016. This time China emerged not as a benefactor to the weak but as a rival to the strong.

In July 2016 the Chinese company Midea bought German technology showpiece Kuka for the record sum of more than €4.5 billion. The Augsburg robot manufacturer was well known to the public. During a state visit by President Obama, just a few months before the takeover, proud German newspapers had published a photo of a Kuka robot tapping a beer for the chancellor and her American guest. The Kuka-shock was followed by a series of Chinese investments and attempted take-overs of top German companies. From 2016 on, German businesspeople – like their colleagues in the US – recognized

---

* In vain the Greek port approached colleagues in Rotterdam, Europe's largest port, as well as the finance ministry in The Hague, to ask whether the Dutch might want to get in ahead of the Chinese. There was no follow-up.

the new reality: Beijing is serious about its strategy, adopted in 2015, of attempting to become a world leader in IT, artificial intelligence, robotics, space travel and more.

Only when Germany fell prey to China was there a joint European response. Prompted by a letter to the Commission from the German, French and Italian economy ministers, a mechanism was put in place – at lightning speed by EU standards – for screening foreign investments (2017–19). In accordance with the mores of rules-politics, the People's Republic was not named, but the geo-economic objective of the legislation was clear to everyone.

The pandemic of 2020 caused a third shock, which heightened public awareness of China's geopolitical power and assertiveness. This time it went far beyond informed or interested circles and was felt right at the heart of European public life. This time, after all, Europe's own medical vulnerability was in the spotlight.

These changed relationships were immediately expressed in the allocation of political responsibility: China became a *Chefsache*. Because of Covid travel restrictions, the summit of all 27 EU government leaders with President Xi that Chancellor Merkel had arranged for September 2020 in Leipzig had not gone ahead. Yet their thinking moved on. In early October, presidents and prime ministers unanimously endorsed the aim of "strategic autonomy".[15] A remarkable conceptual breakthrough, since the notion had for years met resistance from member countries that, in a defence context, considered it anti-Atlantic. Now the medical vulnerability and pharmaceutical dependency revealed by the pandemic prompted calls for an escape from the Chinese-American squeeze. Suddenly an independent foreign policy emerged as a public matter.

In the Union the Covid crisis has reinforced the desire for a "strategic" economic, competition and industrial policy. The realization is dawning that the safeguarding of interests demands more than a free-market framework. This is clearly felt not just in Paris (where such thinking was never absent) but in Berlin, Brussels and even The Hague (traditionally reliant on the market's invisible hand). An historic turning point.

For centuries Europe has operated an offensive trade policy, focused on the opening up of foreign markets. In that connection the contemporary WTO rules for a "level playing field" are the respectable successor to the old gunboat diplomacy. Currently the need for a defensive strategy is making itself felt, since other powers now determine on which playing fields Europe must defend its well-being, economy and ambition.

China's assertive self-consciousness takes some getting used to for societies like those of Europe, which see themselves as the centre of the world and the measure of all things, and which have barely been challenged on those points since 1800. The pandemic has indisputably opened the eyes of the European public. China is changing the nineteenth- and twentieth-century world order substantially. The country's economic strategy is of a kind that Europe is unused to recognizing in powers other than itself, or the US; in the eyes of all those other powers, however, it is nothing new, except that the roles have been reversed. This requires self-reflection by the European Union, reorientation and a reconsideration of the rules of the geopolitical game.

The pandemic crisis highlights three fundamental characteristics of China as a strategic player.[16] First: long-term thinking. As a large, populous civilization, its political culture thinks in epochs, in decades and centuries, instead of counting individual years and paying heed to electoral cycles. When European leaders talk in Beijing about the discomfort of losing hegemony after three centuries, they are told, "For seventeen centuries before that, we were the largest economy".[17] From the perspective of the Chinese, the Covid crisis is a mere ripple, its official death toll of 3,600 a minor misfortune.* This temporal scope applies to both the past and the future. Xi Jinping is focusing on 2049, the centenary of the red revolution, by which time the country intends to be an economic, technological and scientific world power (with Taiwan under its sway).

Second: centralism. The Chinese Communist Party is more powerful than the state. Xi is first of all secretary-general of the CCP, secondly commander-in-chief and only then president – his function for acting on the world stage. The Party controls the state apparatus, the army and all state-owned enterprises, and exercises considerable influence on private companies. Admittedly, censorship and a lack of free media put Beijing on the back foot when Covid first broke out (bad news does not get through), but centralism also enabled the leadership to give the public inside and outside China a single message.

Third: an integrated vision. In Chinese decision-making, political, economic and security dimensions are regarded as a single whole. In the domestic economy this expresses itself in a form of mercantile state capitalism, with diffuse borderlines between state and private companies. The Belt and Road strategy is a perfect example of Chinese foreign policy, which smoothly mixes economic aspects with political and

---

* Asked about the danger of a destructive nuclear war, Mao Zedong once answered: a few hundred million dead is surmountable; we shall withdraw to the Chinese interior and begin again.

military ambitions and, where useful, with a dash of culture or with flattery.* The New Silk Road is both a grand strategy and a networking initiative. Its fluidity is clearly visible in the pandemic's face-mask and vaccine diplomacy, an interplay of strategic thinking, tactical operation and improvisational action.

These three advantages give China a huge capacity to set strategic priorities and immediately put them into practice. The long-term perspective engenders self-confidence, while centralism and an integrated vision enable its translation into immediate action. The size of the country, moreover, ensures that everything it does has consequences for other international players. Thus the international order can be rearranged.

In essence China is copying the global strategy of twentieth-century America in the twenty-first century. The Pax Sinica. The US too, after all, connected and still connects economy and strategy, trade, cultural influence and geopolitics, both visibly and candidly. Europe, by contrast, divides up choices across separate policy domains and its many actors, thereby sabotaging any chance of an effective performance as a geostrategic player.

---

* On a state visit to Athens in 2019, Xi wholeheartedly supported his Greek hosts in their fight for the return of the Elgin Marbles, looted art in the British trophy cabinet. From 1801 onwards the ancient marble frieze was taken from the Acropolis by Lord Elgin, father of the man who ransacked the summer palace. For years the Greeks have been demanding the treasures, now in the British Museum, be returned. Further stirring this feud brought Xi sympathy from the Greeks, his bridgehead for the Silk Road. It also enabled Beijing to pose as the avenger of Western colonial crimes, a discourse that goes down well in Africa, Asia and South America. In the Greek newspaper *Kathimerini*, the president stressed the similarities between the two countries as "ancient civilizations", deploying the slogan, "You have Socrates, we have Confucius".

Yet in the European Union an awareness is dawning of its own strategic weakness and the need to re-evaluate its China policy. In the spring of 2019, a year before the coronavirus outbreak, the European Union produced a remarkable strategic document that did not go unnoticed in Beijing. It defines three roles that China plays for Europe and the European Union. China is a partner in making global aims a reality, such as climate policy, nuclear non-proliferation or the tackling of pandemics. China is a competitor in the economic and technological fields. Finally, China and the EU are "systemic rivals" in the sense that they embody alternative political models, with the Union attaching far greater value to individual rights and democratic institutions.

That third role, the one that causes the most diplomatic headaches, is essential for the Union's self-image and the determining of its position between the great powers. Thirty years after the fall of the Berlin Wall and Fukuyama's announcement of "the end of history", Europe is dispensing with the idea that liberal democracy is the destination for all the states and civilizations of the world. But there is a snag. Those who see a "systemic rival" must also look at themselves. Those who recognize that not everyone in the world has to become the same can no longer make do with a self-image that claims to be based on universal values. And if China manifests itself as a civilization and a great power, then which narrative, which self-image and which power is Europe able or willing to set against it?

The shocks experienced by Europeans since 2008 with regard to China, which have reached their provisional high-point in the pandemic, are probably only the start. How the next act in this geopolitical drama will unfold will be decided by the way each of the two relates to the third player in the triangle: the US.

After the Pax Americana

In 1917 the American Republic set foot on European soil for the first time as a power among powers. US energy and troop numbers hastened the end of the horrors of trench warfare. But as early as 1920 – also the year in which the pandemic fevers of the Spanish influenza subsided – the Senate called a halt to such internationalism and America's first European adventure abruptly ended.

Things went rather differently after the Second World War. America's role as an ally against the Nazis and an occupying power flowed seamlessly into that of being a defender against the new enemy, Russia, in Western and Southern Europe at least. From 1945 onwards it was an enduring imperial power on the continent. After the collapse of the Soviet empire in 1989–91 the sway of the United States was extended further eastwards. European governments accepted the loss of their own geopolitical capacity to act. This unique bond between great power and protégé has been described as "empire by invitation".[18]

There are two sides to the Pax Americana: global public good and self-interest. International agreements and organizations like the United Nations promote freedom and prosperity and temper raw power politics, which explains why the system was praised in Western Europe as the "international", "multilateral", "liberal" or "rules-based" order. In Washington there was also talk of the "American-led" order, a term that describes the power relationship rather better. After all, the UN has its headquarters in New York, while the International Monetary Fund and the World Bank have theirs in Washington, DC, and the dollar is the cornerstone of the system.

The rise of China as a rival is straining this 70-year-old order. For Washington it represents a geopolitical challenge that puts everything else in the shade. Step by step, the consequences for European-American relations are becoming visible.

Already under President Obama, the US started its "pivot to Asia", an orientation towards the Pacific. The aim was to station 60 per cent of the overseas American air force and navy in Asia, while the military presence in Europe would be cut back. To curb China's dominance in East Asia, the US offered its neighbouring countries protection. Since 2010 the American navy has pointedly patrolled the South China Sea, provoking China to build its first aircraft carriers. In parallel, Obama worked on a trade agreement with a group of Asian countries that excluded China. True, this Trans Pacific Partnership (TPP) ran aground in Congress in 2016, but that does not alter the fact of the geopolitical turn towards the Pacific. The European theatre has been relegated to the side-stage of world politics for the first time in centuries. The European players are now to their surprise more like extras on the global stage than leads.

Under President Trump, the deterioration in the relationship between America and China accelerated. In August 2018 the president signed a law that made China a policy priority; to retain its geopolitical primacy, the US allowed itself to deploy all available means, economic and military included.

Early in his term of office Trump unleashed a trade war with China. After a while, the US – shaken awake by Xi's ten-year plan *Made in China 2025* – started targeting high-value technology companies such as telecoms giant Huawei. Washington put European and other allies under pressure to isolate China. As a result of the 2020 pandemic, this rivalry permeated all the way to the main podium of global public life, with a furious narrative battle, a geo-medical vaccine race and a tug of war in the WHO. At home it was the American secretary of defense who dotted the "i"s and crossed the "t"s. Shortly before the 2020 presidential election he decreed that from 2021 onwards, military academies must devote half their lessons to China.[19] In the American imagination the People's Liberation Army is conclusively the strategic and narrative successor to the Russian Red Army. There was a new Cold War in the making.

In the Trump years the European public underwent a discontinuity experience of its own. For the first time since Harry S. Truman (1945–53), the White House broke with the fundamentals of the Pax Americana. With his unashamedly economic-nationalist agenda, Trump gave up pretending that America's exercise of power and promotion of stability and freedom were two sides of the same coin. For the president all that mattered was power; other values were subordinate or negotiable. European leaders no longer felt like allies but like vassals, forced to pay protection money. Angela Merkel had every reason to declare, in May 2017, that Europeans need to take destiny "into our own hands". She realized that America's withdrawal was more than a presidential whim. The American people were no longer prepared to pay the price of the Pax element of their country's international leadership, whether in the form of trade agreements that threatened jobs at home or in the form of distant wars that cost the lives of their sons or daughters. It was precisely this change that Trump's election laid bare. His America First was less "isolationism" than anti-imperialism from the centre.

Confronted with this double legacy, Joe Biden – the new president of an America shaken by the pandemic – opted in early 2021 for both continuity and rupture. He could not avoid further pursuing a confrontational course with Xi Jinping. Biden cannot allow himself a meek stance in the face of China's expansionary power, but he is breaking with the policy of inconveniencing and weakening allies and international organizations, and positioning the US once again as the self-conscious leader of the free world. All the same, it will be harder for him than for his postwar predecessors to make self-interest and global interests credibly coincide, because of both the reluctance of his voters and the relative decline of America's power.

Seen like this, rupture and continuity have the same origin. Because of the mounting geopolitical conflict with China, Joe Biden is playing the card of American imperialism: "Our power is your freedom". The US realizes that against this challenger it cannot win on its own. In early 2019 Biden's current secretary of state Antony Blinken was already making a start, with a plea for a "league of democracies" (a proposal he made along with neoconservative Robert Kagan).[20] Biden announced a "Summit of Democracies" to be held during his first year in office. In Washington the narrative of a new Cold War is developing, in which the power struggle with Beijing is amplified into a battle between Good and Evil. The European democracies, naturally, are cast on the side of the Good.

This is in stark contrast to China's approach to Europe. Whereas Xi Jinping always talks of the relationship with the US as being between great powers, with Europe he stresses the bond between "great civilizations". He claims that China is the oldest still extant civilization, representing "the East", whereas the origins of Western civilization lie in Europe. Because of that historical responsibility, Xi believes, China and Europe must work together to build a world in which all states, irrespective of their political-economic systems, have equal standing. As well as China and Europe (with a special emphasis on Greece), India and Egypt are also among the "ancient civilizations". So, between Scylla and Charybdis, Europe will have to formulate a strategic autonomy that can withstand the temptations and is able to take a role on the world stage.

The initial reflex of governments and EU institutions after the 2020 American presidential election was to reach out a hand to Joe Biden in relief, almost before he had stretched out a hand to them.[21] Yet a number of crucial differences between this and the previous Cold War should give us pause.

New is the degree of global economic interdependence, of which the pandemic is the viral counterpart. Globalization, which started with the opening up of China's economy, beginning in 1978 and accelerating from the 1990s onwards, changes the stakes of the geopolitical conflict. The US and the Soviet Union engaged in an ideological and territorial battle, with famous flashpoints including Berlin, Cuba and Vietnam. Economic links between the capitalist West and the Eastern Bloc were minimal, however, and as a consequence it cost Western Europe little to restrict trade and transactions with the communist bloc. How different the situation is now. The rapid global spread of the coronavirus has revealed how immensely branched and interwoven worldwide supply chains have become. To disentangle them in a process of decoupling, as American hardliners advocate, would be economically disastrous for Europe – leaving aside the question of whether it is possible at all.

Furthermore, America's disconcerting Covid response reveals how weakened, divided and embittered the country is, and indeed how self-conscious and resolute the onward march of China. At its height the Soviet Union achieved 60 per cent of American prosperity, whereas now China might well catch up with the US in the foreseeable future, not just economically but technologically and militarily. Whereas immediately after the Second World War the US accounted for around half of the world's prosperity, it currently accounts for just one seventh. The days of global supremacy are now out of reach to *both* those great imperial powers. This creates a need for forms of power balance and coexistence – and hence thinking in terms of pluralism.

The European Union derives part of its self-confidence and sense of mission from the notion of a universal, neutral and power-free international podium. With the pandemic and the resulting politicization of the WHO and UN by Beijing and Washington, that promise has been shattered. The Union, still gasping for breath, therefore needs not only to prop up the multilateral order (impossible without the bedrock of American power) but to promote a multipolar order. This means the Union must first develop the ambition to be a relevant pole itself, a power among powers. Only then will Europe be taken seriously by the US and China as a fellow player on the world stage.

Such a geopolitical aspiration requires – this much is made clear by the American example and the Chinese counterexample – a strategic capacity to prioritize, buttressed by a public will to operate as a unified Europe, to act, to claim a certain space. To that end Europe must free itself from the role of a prompt that invisibly declaims universal values or the agreements of rules-politics. A player on the stage accepts being absorbed into the stream of events and into a battle for soil, technology, access, influence and prestige – and must speak the language of fellow players, the language of power.[22] This change of role is radical; scripts from the previous role offer no direction. In the new division of roles, improvisation is unavoidable.

In liberal democracies this turnaround cannot be the result of a top-down decision. It will take place as a gradual shift driven by many public choices. One of the three great assets of China's geopolitical development, centralist decisiveness, is therefore beyond Europe's reach. There is no reason to deplore this, since freedom and pluralism are great strengths. But the other two assets, historical consciousness and an integrated strategic vision, can and should certainly be deployed.

Europe as a whole has an historical and cultural identity on which rests a story of its own; to all observers outside the continent this is obvious. What remains to be found is the will, or the capacity, of Europe to give this narrative political shape. The lure of universalism is strong, as is the temptation to be absorbed into a "West" that includes the US and Canada. But global power relations have simply changed; that is what the pandemic has revealed. A clear and strong self-image therefore demands a twofold narrative emancipation. On the one hand the powerful pole that is Xi's China has "provincialized" universalism,* while on the other hand the self-interest of Trump's America has broken the narrative spell of "the West". After the years 2016–20 it will be difficult for Europeans ever again to believe in the promise of the Pax Americana – although the compelling effect of the narrative machine that is Washington and Hollywood in creating a new enemy should not be underestimated.

More is said in the Union about a strategic vision, the third great challenge, than about the historical consciousness of a community of destiny. The need to integrate political, economic and cultural interests into a single vision has been recognized for several years, not least because of the challenge of China. Geopolitical criteria are employed alongside appraisals of commercial and financial interests. The obstacles are, of course, formidable, not merely because of fragmented policy in the Union but mainly because member states define their strategic interests differently. For instance, when France mobilized against Islamist terror in the Sahel with military action for reasons of Europe's security (and even though it did so with troops from the Netherlands, Denmark and Estonia), a significant portion of the German public regarded that same action as neocolonialist and as a misplaced expression of past grandeur. There is no need to multiply examples of how geographical and historical experiences vary.

What has become necessary for Europe as a whole is a strategic conversation at the highest political level about its

---

* Strengthened by America's pandemic implosion, Chinese intellectuals loyal to the government said to the *New York Times* in the summer of 2020, "Back when I was weak, I had to totally play by your rules. Now I'm strong and have confidence, so why can't I lay down my own rules and values and ideas?"

shared aims and interests, about its place in space and in time. This will force a continent that after 1945 escaped from the morass of self-destruction by mentally clinging to universal values, borderless space and abstract time to re-engage with geography and history in the full sense of the word. Between what powers on the map do we find ourselves, and between what past and what future? The US is reinventing itself as a Pacific power. Instead of being the eastern side of the Atlantic order, Europe will in the future occupy Eurasia's western reaches, the largest land area on the planet at whose edge lies the Chinese economic giant. Positioned on the northern shore of the Mediterranean, it will feel its proximity to fast-growing Africa ever more strongly. Reorientation is required.[23]

It should preferably happen before Lady Fortune comes to point a finger at the continent's vulnerabilities. Over the past few years, unsettling events on the external borders have at long last persuaded member states of their shared destiny. In the conflict over Ukraine (2014–15) the entire Union backed robust action against Russia in the form of unanimously agreed economic sanctions, which have been extended every six months since. It was not until the refugee crisis of 2015–16 that the Northern European public recognized the Mediterranean as de facto Europe's southern border and (all too modest) first steps were taken towards jointly getting to grips with the phenomenon of migration. The insular British secession (2016–20) also necessitated combined action and a united front.

In 2020 the pandemic inferno and the Covid battle between great powers opened the eyes of the European public to its own vulnerability. Strategic autonomy is a first, necessary response. At the same time, the political leadership in Berlin and Paris realizes that military and nuclear dependence on the US cannot be reversed in the blink of an eye. Some believe that Europe's limited resources and capabilities make any conversation about strategic aims futile.[24] It is a misapprehension that may have serious consequences. History marches on; the pandemic throws the prospects of bitter geopolitical isolation into sharp relief. Europe's strategic turn demands a self-conscious script, a purposeful direction and a recognition of historical interconnectedness. Only based on shared political self-confidence will the European public be prepared to send its political representatives out into the world to demand a relevant role "in Europe's name" in the conflict of geopolitical interests that is flaring up.

Perhaps the Biden presidency will give Europeans some breathing space, after four years of Trump, in which to begin this strategic task, to safeguard their shared existence as a democracy, a civilization and a body politic. But time does not stand still. Once the pandemic and its aftershocks are behind us, new and old crises within and without will continue to pummel European societies. The era in which security, prosperity and liberty were available cost free is over. At times events will force the European public and its politicians to acknowledge tragic choices, and their Union to start operating strategically. Ultimately, this, too, is about saving Europe.

Notes

PROLOGUE: PANIC

1. "Urbi et Orbi message of his holiness Pope Francis", 12 April 2020.
2. Cited in Elise Ann Allen, "Cardinal fears coronavirus could be end of European Union", *Crux*, 17 April 2020.
3. Jacques Delors, 18 March 2020, cited in Thomas Wieder, Jean-Pierre Stroobants and Virginie Malingre, "Coronavirus: Les divisions de l'Union européenne la placent face à un 'danger mortel'", *Le Monde*, 1 April 2020.
4. Thomas Mayer, "Juncker: 'Nach der Krise werden wir bessere Europäer sein'", *Der Standard*, 9 April 2020.
5. Mario Draghi, "We face a war against coronavirus and must mobilise accordingly", *Financial Times*, 25 March 2020.
6. Wolfgang Münchau, "How the next euro crisis could unfold", *Financial Times*, 12 April 2020.
7. Cited in Hans von der Burchard, "Italy's Conte warns of EU collapse ahead crucial financial talks", Politico.eu, 9 April 2020.
8. European Commission, "Spring 2020 Economic Forecast: a deep and uneven recession, an uncertain recovery", 6 May 2020.
9. The report, first placed on the website of the Chinese embassy in Paris and entitled "Rétablir des faits distordus: observations d'un diplomate chinois en poste à Paris" is no longer available there. For the official protest by the French government, see n.n., "L'ambassadeur de Chine à Paris convoqué pour 'certains propos' liés au coronavirus", in *Le Monde*, 15 April 2020.
10. Compare n.n., "Russian senator falsely claims Poles closed airspace to virus aid", in Polygraph.info, 24 March 2020; compare for the outcome and further events n.n., "Coronavirus disinformation: Moscow overplays its hand", EUvsDisinfo, 8 April 2020.

11. Dante Alighieri, *The Divine Comedy*, XXXIV lines 135–9, trans. C. H. Sisson (New York: Oxford University Press, 1980). (Completed 1320. First published in Italian as *Comedia* in 1472).

1 THE EXPERIENCE OF A CRISIS

1. Daniel Defoe, *A Journal of the Plague Year*, Lector House 2019, 14. (First published 1722).
2. Paul Krugman, "Apocalypse fairly soon", *New York Times*, 17 May 2012; Willem Buiter, cited in Cheyenne Hopkins and Tom Keene, "Citigroup's Buiter says Europe must stop default now", Bloomberg, 16 November 2011.
3. Jean-Claude Juncker in his New Year press conference, 15 January 2016, available via YouTube.
4. Defoe, *A Journal*, 14. (Although Defoe published the book in 1722, more than half a century after the events, during which he was five years old, he carried out research seriously and may have based the book on his uncle's plague year diaries.)
5. Victor Mallet and Roula Khalaf, "Emmanuel Macron: 'we are at a moment of truth'", *Financial Times*, 17 April 2020.
6. J. K. Rowling, "On monsters, villains and the EU referendum", June 2016; https://www.jkrowling.com/opinions/monsters-villains-eu-referendum.
7. Thomas Friedman, "Our new historical divide: BC and AC – the world before corona and the world after", *New York Times*, 17 March 2020.
8. Ivan Krastev, *Is It Tomorrow Yet? Paradoxes of the Pandemic* (London: Allen Lane, 2020).
9. Art. 6(a) TFEU; art. 168 TFEU.
10. Olga Tokarczuk, "Jetzt kommen neue Zeiten!", *Frankfurter Allgemeine Zeitung*, 31 March 2020.
11. Simon Jenkins, "The coronavirus crisis has exposed the truth about the EU: it's not a real union", *The Guardian*, 10 April 2020.
12. Nils Minkmar, "Europa in der Corona-Krise: was für eine Enttäuschung", *Der Spiegel*, 17 March 2020.
13. Luuk van Middelaar, *The Passage to Europe: How a Continent Became a Union* (London: Yale University Press, 2013), 11–33. (Originally published as Luuk van Middelaar, *De passage naar Europa. Geschiedenis van een begin*, Groningen: Historische Uitgeverij, 2009).

2 METAMORPHOSIS:
A DIFFERENT HISTORY OF THE UNION

1. Martin Luther, *Werke*, part 41 (sermon of 10 May 1535) (Weimar, 1910), 138.

2. For the medieval monarch there was already a spectrum from *jurisdictio* (the declaring of the law) to *gubernaculum* (the control of the rudder); from the appeal to custom or an advisory council to the lonely, rapid decision. See J. G. A. Pocock, *The Machiavellian Moment: Florentine Political Thought and the Atlantic Republican Tradition* (Princeton, NJ: Princeton University Press, 1975), 26.

3. Covered in detail in my *The Passage to Europe*, especially chapters 4 and 5 (founding years and post-1989 "Wende" years respectively) and my *Alarums and Excursions: Improvising Politics on the European Stage* (Newcastle upon Tyne: Agenda, 2019) (crisis years since 2008).

4. Reinhart Koselleck, *Sediments of Time* (Stanford, CA: Stanford University Press, 2018), 9. (Originally published as *Zeitschichten. Studien zur Historik*, Frankfurt: Suhrkamp, 2000).

5. For a distinction in this connection between "technical", "procedural" and "constitutional" depoliticization, see *Alarums and Excursions*, 222–7.

6. Paul-Henri Spaak, January 1962, cited in Anthony Teasdale, "The Fouchet Plan: De Gaulle's Intergovernmental Design for Europe", *LEQS Paper* no. 117, 1.

7. For the first assessment, see for example, Jacques Delors, "Discours lors de la remise de la médaille de la Paix de Nimègue", 15 March 2010, 10 (www.institutdelors.eu) and Jürgen Habermas, *Zur Verfassung Europas. Ein Essay* (Frankfurt: Suhrkamp, 2011). For the second, see Herman Van Rompuy, "Discours à Sciences-Po Paris", 20 September 2010.

8. 1995 saw the accession of Sweden, Finland and Austria, three countries that were neutral in the Cold War, situated in the area between the two blocs.

9. Éric Bussière and Vincent Dujardin, "Entretien avec Jacques Delors" (unpublished), recorded 13 January 2016 in Paris as part of the book project, *The European Commission 1986–2000: History and Memories of an Institution* (Luxembourg: EU Publications Office, 2019).

10. Angela Merkel, "Rede der Bundeskanzlerin anlässlich der Eröffnung des. 61. Akademischen Jahres des Europakollegs Brügge", 2 November 2010.

11. Manuel Sarrazin and Sven-Christian Kindler, "'Brügge sehen und sterben': Gemeinschaftsmethode versus Unionsmethode", in *integration* 35 (2012) 3, 214–23. Both members of the Bundestag for the Green party concluded (223) "The route according to the Bruges Method, however, might be fatal for the European Union, as was the stay in Bruges for many protagonists in the film".

12. While the Community and the Union existed in parallel after the Maastricht Union Treaty (1993) took effect, the Lisbon Treaty legally dissolved the Community and gave the Union legal personality. On that occasion the Community Treaty was renamed the Treaty on the Functioning of the European Union (TFEU), which exists alongside the Treaty on European Union (TEU).

13. Pocock, *The Machiavellian Moment*, viii.

ENTR'ACTE: A PUBLIC AFFAIR

1. Albert Camus, *The Plague*, trans. Stuart Gilbert (London: Penguin, 1960 [1948]), 57. (Originally published as *La Peste*, Paris, 1947).

2. World Health Organization, "Listings of WHO's response to COVID-19"; https://www.who.int/news/item/29-06-2020-covidtimeline.

3. John Dewey, *The Public and its Problems: An Essay in Political Inquiry* (Athens, OH: Ohio University Press, 1954), 12.

4. Dewey, *The Public*, 62.

5. Dewey, *The Public*, 31.

6. Apart from the national "no" to new treaties voiced through the ballot box in Denmark, France, the Netherlands and Ireland (or against the euro, in Sweden in 2003), we might also consider the unexpressed refusal of the European public to agree to Turkish accession to the Union. This signal was received in the 2000s, first by the government leaders (candidate Sarkozy made it the central theme of his campaign in the French presidential election of 2007). It is nevertheless revealing to see how the Brussels machinery, as ever, translated this purely political cry into a technocratic criterion, the newly invented "absorption capacity" of the union. After the major enlargement of 2004, until further notice no one else would fit in, so to speak. For a detailed analysis of this territorial depoliticization strategy, see Hans Kribbe, *The Strongmen: European Encounters with Sovereign Power* (Newcastle upon Tyne: Agenda, 2020), 142–5.

3   CHRONICLE OF THE CORONAVIRUS CRISIS

1. The image of concentric circles is adapted from Jeremy Farrar, "The worst of Covid-19 may still be to come", *Financial Times*, 21 July 2020.

2. See (for the call by Kyriakides) David M. Herszenhorn and Sarah Wheaton, "How Europe failed the corona test", Politico.eu, 7 April 2020; (for Speranza) n.n. "Italian health minister: Coronavirus is not a justifiable reason to reintroduce Schengen borders", in Schengenvisainfo.com, 12 February 2020; and (for Buzyn and Spahn) Spahn's tweet of 4 February 2020 (13:13), after a bilateral meeting in Paris.

3. Council of the European Union, Conclusions Covid-19 (13 February 2020), point 15.

4. Spanish prime minister Pablo Sanchez frankly admitted as much on 14 July 2020 in Berlin. "We thought this pandemic would perhaps affect many in Asia or Africa, but a system like ours, a community system like ours, would somehow be spared, not suffering any pandemic, the way it often or almost systematically happens on other continents. That was a lesson". The statement is available in German on the Federal Chancellery's website.

5. The image is that of Chef de clinique Dr Renneboog of the Molière hospital in Brussels (conversation with the author on 31 July 2020).

6. De Block on Twitter, 6 March 2020 (12:36).

7. The various press conferences and statements before and after the meeting are available online: https://newsroom.consilium.europa.eu/events/20200303-extraordinary-employment-social-policy-health-and-consumer-affairs-council-health-march-2020.

8. Maurizio Massari, "Italian Ambassador to the EU: Italy needs Europe's help", Politico.eu, 10 March 2020.

9. Dutch Ministry of Health, Welfare and Sport, letter dated 19 May 2020 in answer to a question in parliament by Lilianne Ploumen (PvdA) about European tendering for medical equipment and supplies.

10. See the European Commission press release "Coronavirus: Commission bid to ensure supply of personal protective equipment for the EU proves successful", 24 March 2020.

11. Joint statement by the Members of the European Council, 26 March 2020, point 5: "We call on the Commission to continue and accelerate its efforts to help ensuring urgent and adequate

provision of medical equipment throughout the EU, which is the most acute priority".

12. See press release "COVID-19: Commission creates first ever rescEU stockpile of medical equipment", 19 March 2020.

13. Imperial College COVID-19 Response Team, "Impact of non-pharmaceutical interventions (NPIs) to reduce COVID-19 mortality and healthcare demand", 16 March 2020.

14. David M. Herszenhorn and Sarah Wheaton, "How Europe failed the corona test", Politico.eu, 7 April 2020.

15. Elena Sánchez Nicolás, "EU experts: closing borders 'ineffective' for coronavirus", EUobserver, 28 February 2020; Nicolás, "Coronavirus: EU at high risk amid global panic", EUobserver, 3 March 2020.

16. While "public policy and the internal security of the Member States" are given as grounds for closing the external borders ("Schengen Border Code", 2016), public health is given as a reason only for refusing access to an individual.

17. See "Guidelines for border management measures to protect health and ensure the availability of goods and essential services", 16 March 2021.

18. Politico spoke of a "near-death experience": Paola Tamma and Hanne Cokelaere, "Schengen proves hard to reboot after system meltdown", Politico.eu, 12 May 2020.

19. Alberto Alemanno, "We lived the European dream. Will any politician stand up for open borders?", *The Guardian*, 22 May 2020. See also Alemanno, "We urgently need a coordinated European response to coronavirus", *EuroNews*, 19 March 2020.

20. Communication from the Commission, "Towards a phased and coordinated approach for restoring freedom of movement and lifting internal border controls – COVID-19" (2020/C 169/03).

21. See n.n., "Poland to join Baltic travel bubble next week", Kafkadesk, 5 June 2020.

22. Cited in Terje Solsvik and Jacob Gronholt-Pedersen, "Sweden excluded as neighbours Denmark and Norway ease travel restrictions", Reuters, 29 May 2020.

23. Cited in Cristina Gonzalez, "Don't treat Italy as a leper colony due to coronavirus, says minister", Politico.eu, 30 May 2020.

24. Cited in n.n., "Poland to join Baltic travel bubble next week", Kafkadesk, 5 June 2020.

25. Commissioner Johansson's speech, delivered on 7 May 2020; https://ec.europa.eu/commission/commissioners/2019-2024/

johansson/announcements/opening-statement-commissioner-johansson-schengen-migration-and-asylum-policy-and-eu-security_en.

26. Monnet, 1953, as recalled by E. P. Wellenstein, 13 August 2008, conversation with the author, cited in Van Middelaar, *The Passage to Europe* (Prologue).

27. Charles Michel, "Europe brings home over half a million stranded citizens. An unprecedented challenge!" European Council press release, 15 May 2020.

28. Matina Stevis-Gridneff, "E.U. may bar American travellers as it reopens borders, citing failures on virus", *New York Times*, 24 June 2020.

29. See "Coronavirus panic stunning market declines fan recession fears", *Washington Post*, 9 March 2020.

30. Christine Lagarde, 12 March, press conference verbatim available online. Lagarde attempted to rectify her blunder afterwards in haste with an interview on CNBC, of which the reassuring core sentence was added as a footnote to the official transcript of the press conference.

31. Sergio Mattarelli, cited in Martin Arnold and Tommy Stubbington, "Lagarde triggers investors jitters as ECB launches virus response", *Financial Times*, 12 March 2020.

32. Press release 18 March 2020: "ECB announces €750 billion Pandemic Emergency Purchase Programme (PEPP)".

33. Christine Lagarde, "Our response to the coronavirus emergency", 19 March 2020. The first package was indeed increased on 4 June 2020 by €600 billion.

34. Jérôme Batout, "La résolution, historique, d'émettre une dette européenne mutualisée sur les marchés financiers est le signal que quelque chose a changé", *Le Monde*, 12 June 2020.

35. To be more precise, the ECB can help to absorb a supply shock only to a limited extent (for example with more favourable interest rates and investment conditions for the industry), but it can do rather more about a demand shock (especially if the unconventional measure of "helicopter money" is deployed, directly or via the banks, to individual households). Nonetheless, in a situation where interest rates are already historically low or even negative, and with huge programmes of quantitative easing, the margins are minimal and negative side-effects (for example through uncertainty for private banks) real. So the main responsibility of the ECB lies with the mitigating of the third major risk, financial uncertainty in the markets. While Lagarde

was right to point out the responsibility of governments for problems one and two, she failed on the third.

36. The first budgetary stimulus was announced by the German government on 9 March, with further announcements on 13, 23, 24 and 27 March 2020. Until early August this was a matter of a direct stimulus of 8.3 per cent of GNP, 7.3 per cent in delayed payments and more than 24 per cent in liquidity and bank guarantees, by far the largest figures in Europe. See the overview by Julia Anderson *et al.*, "The fiscal response to the economic fallout from the coronavirus", 5 August 2020, available online.

37. Cited in Politico.eu, 9 March 2020.

38. Commission press release dated 20 March 2020 about the Stability and Growth Pact. Agreement by the Eurogroup was reached on 23 March. Compare Eurogroup press release of 16 March 2020, available online. "The SGP has the flexibility needed to cater for this situation and we will make full use of this flexibility in all member states".

39. To be more precise, they came together as the Eurogroup in both an "inclusive format" (27, with non-eurozone guests) and the regular format (eurozone ministers).

40. The Commission came up with €65 billion in subsidies for affected governments, while the European Investment Bank mobilized €20 billion in credit guarantees for up to 150,000 companies and promised another €20 billion in business investment.

41. Conclusions of the European Council, 26 March 2020.

42. António Costa cited by Natasha Donn, Portugal Resident, 27 March 2020, available at https://www.portugalresident.com/repugnant-pm-costa-launches-extraordinary-attack-on-dutch-finance-minister/

43. Michaela Wiegel and Konrad Schuller, "Merkel musste, Macron konnte", *Frankfurter Allgemeine Zeitung*, 24 May 2020.

44. Paola Tamma, "EU governments roll back wage support despite corona uncertainty", Politico.eu, 10 August 2020.

45. Angela Merkel, Regierungserklärung, 23 April 2020; https://www.bundeskanzlerin.de/bkin-de/aktuelles/regierungserklaerung-von-bundeskanzlerin-merkel-1746554.

46. Between March and July 2020 the Commission gave the 27 member states the green light for state aid in the order of €2.9 trillion. Of that amount, 58 per cent (!) or around €1.7 trillion, was given by Germany alone to its businesses. See Jade

Grandin de l'Éprevier, "Aides d'État: l'Allemagne fausse-t-elle la concurrence?", *L'Opinion* (30 September 2020); data based on research by the French National Bank. There is no undisputed figure for the cost of German reunification, but for recovery support (excluding welfare) the usual estimate is €300 billion.

47. Budgetary Instrument for Convergence and Competitiveness (BICC). See the report by the French minister of his 2018 battle with his Dutch counterpart in Bruno Le Maire, *Le Nouvel Empire: l'Europe du Vingt-et-Unième Siècle* (Paris: Gallimard, 2019), 33–7.

48. For a glimpse behind the scenes of this dialogue of the deaf, just a few months before the Covid-19 outbreak, see Steven Erlanger, "Merkel and Macron clash publicly over NATO comments", *New York Times*, 23 November 2019.

49. Cited in *Frankfurter Allgemeine Zeitung*, "Merkel musste, Macron konnte", 24 May 2020 (*"ich werde nicht lockerlassen"*).

50. Mallet and Khalaf, "Emmanuel Macron: 'we are at a moment of truth'".

51. Angela Merkel, "Merkel on eurobonds: 'Not in my lifetime'", 26 June 2012, *Euractiv.com*.

52. See David M. Herszenhorn, Jacopo Barigazzi and Rym Momtaz, "Virtual summit, real acrimony: EU leaders clash over 'corona bonds'", Politico.eu, 27 March 2020. Immediately after the letter from the nine, economics minister and Merkel confidant Peter Altmaier called the coronavirus discussion a *"Gespensterdebatte"*, a "ghost debate". See Moritz Koch, Thomas Sigmund and Klaus Stratmann, "Die Diskussion über Euro-Bonds ist eine Gespensterdebatte", *Handelsblatt*, 24 March 2020.

53. Instead the gathered eurozone governments set up stability mechanisms outside the EU treaty (first the EFSF, then the ESM), the former a body governed by private law, the latter a public body, with which they raised money on the financial markets to pay the costs "per head" per member state, in proportion to the GDP-related deposits in the ECB.

54. German diplomat cited in Thomas Wieder and Cécile Boutelet, "Comment Angela Merkel s'est convertie au plan de relance pour éviter l'"effondrement' de l'Europe", *Le Monde*, 17 July 2020.

55. Robin Alexander and Jacques Schuster, "Niemand is vor dem Beifall von der falschen Seite sicher", interview with Wolfgang Schäuble, *Welt am Sonntag*, 24 May 2020.

56. Marc Peeperkorn, "Hoe twee Nederlandse 'wonderkinderen' de architecten van het Europese herstelfonds werden", *de Volkskrant*, 16 July 2020.

57. Quoted in Peeperkorn, "Hoe twee Nederlandse", *de Volkskrant*, 16 July 2020. See also Florian Gathmann *et al.*, "Sie finden einander nicht nur gut", *Spiegel.de*, 15 June 2020.

58. "Non-paper EU support for efficient and sustainable COVID-19 recovery", 23 May 2020, available online.

59. For an overview of bilateral talks see Ralf Drachenberg, "Outcome of the Special European Council meeting of 17–21 July 2020" in European Parliament Research Service Blog, 23 July 2020.

60. See for example Zsolt David, "Having the cake, but slicing it differently: How is the grand EU recovery fund allocated?", Bruegel.org, 23 July 2020.

61. According to Macron at the press conference afterwards.

62. "The European Council underlines the importance of the respect of the rule of law". Everyone felt able to take that sentence home. Conclusions of the European Council 17–21 July 2020, point A24, repeated in Annex, point 22.

63. "Pressekonferenz von Bundeskanzlerin Merkel und Präsident Macron am 21 Juli 2020". English available at https://www. bundesregierung.de/breg-en/news/europaeischer-rat-1770286.

64. Laurenz Gehrke, "How Europe reacted to the new EU budget and coronavirus recovery fund deal", Politico.eu, 21 July 2020.

65. Conclusions of the European Council 17–21 July 2020, Annex, point 145. ("as a first step" there was to be a tax on "non-recycled plastic packaging waste", point 146.)

66. "Statement by His Holiness the Dalai Lama welcoming EU agreement", 22 July 2020.

67. Clara van de Wiel, "Ursula von der Leyen: we staarden in de afgrond", *NRC Handelsblad*, 24 July 2020.

68. Otto Neurath, *Durch die Kriegswirtschaft zur Naturalwirtschaft* (Munich: Callwey, 1919). English translation taken from the chapter "Through war economy to economy in kind" in Otto Neurath, *Empiricism and Sociology*, trans. Paul Foulkes and Marie Neurath (Boston, MA: Reidel, 1973).

69. On 3 March 2020 CureVac CEO Daniel Menichella had an audience with Donald Trump and the US coronavirus working group in the White House, during which he discussed his company's coronavirus vaccine development; https://www.curevac.com/ en/2020/03/03/curevac-ceo-daniel-menichella-discusses-coronavirus-vaccine-development-with-u-s-president-donald-trump-and-members-of-coronavirus-task-force/.

70. "Sanofi et un vaccin contre le Covid-19 en priorité pour les États-Unis: une polémique vite devenue politique en France", *Le Monde*, 14 May 2020.

71. See Dutch government press release dated 13 June 2020, available in English at https://www.government.nl/latest/news/2020/06/13/contract-for-possible-coronavirus-vaccine-for-europe.

72. Cited in n.n. "Maggie De Block juge déraisonnable de négocier un vaccin en dehors de l'initiative européenne", *Le Soir*, 13 June 2020.

73. Stéphane Alonso, "Nederland investeert niet meer met kopgroep in ontwikkeling coronavaccin", *NRC Handelsblad*, 17 June 2020.

74. When criticism concerning the vaccine mandate first arose, in early 2021, the Commission pointed to the informal European Council of 19 June 2020 (see "Questions & Answers on vaccine negotiations", 8 January 2021). But there are no written conclusions available for that video summit, and during the press conference afterwards neither of the presidents, Michel and Von der Leyen, said a word on the subject of vaccines. The agreement between the Commission and the participating member states, which presumes a mandate, dates from 18 June – the day before the meeting – and points to a Council regulation of 14 April 2020 that activated an emergency support mechanism. The matter was probably decided between 13 and 17 June in a number of phone calls between Berlin, Paris, The Hague, Rome and Brussels.

75. Jasmin Bauomy, "Coronavirus: EU says it struck deal with Sanofi for 300 million doses of potential COVID-19 vaccine", euronews.com, 31 July 2020.

76. Katja Gloger and Georg Mascolo, *Ausbruch: Innenansichten einer Pandemie* (Munich: Piper, 2021), 236–46.

77. "Press conference by Charles Michel, Ursula von der Leyen and Angela Merkel", Brussels, 11 December 2020 (video available at: https://www.consilium.europa.eu/en/media-galleries/european-council/meetings/2020-12-10-euco/?slide=5).

78. Markus Becker *et al.*, "The planning disaster. Germany and Europe could fall short on vaccine supplies", *Spiegel International*, 18 December 2020. The accusations were denied by the Commission.

79. Gloger and Mascolo, *Ausbruch*, 245.

80. See Tony Connelly, "EU vaccine roll-out – the needle and the damage done", RTÉ.ie, 1 April 2021.

81. Clive Cookson, "UK vaccine supremo Kate Bingham: 'The bickering needs to stop'", *Financial Times*, 3 April 2020.

82. Slovakia's Prime Minister Igor Matovic on 7 February in *Le Monde*: "Personally, I think the Commission did a good job. I hardly dare imagine in which situation Slovakia would find itself had we not been part of the European Union".

83. Charlemagne, "The EU should stop ignoring the vaccine race to try and win it", *Economist.com*, 21 January 2021.

84. For the situation in Poland, see Ekke Overbeek, "Staatscorruptie met EU-geld. Europa faciliteert de Poolse antidemocratie", *De Groene Amsterdammer*, 5 May 2021.

85. Eszter Zalan, "First recovery euros could be paid out in July", *EUobserver*, 11 May 2021.

4   A PUBLIC THEATRE

1. Alexis de Tocqueville, *Democracy in America* (New York: Knopf, 1956), 112. (Originally published as *De la démocratie en Amérique*, Paris, 1835/1840).

2. Miles Johnson *et al.*, "Coronavirus: Is Europe losing Italy?", *Financial Times*, 6 April 2020.

3. In late 2018 the fiscally conservative chief economist and former Schäuble confidant Ludger Schauknecht left the German finance ministry. Under minister Olaf Scholz he was succeeded by former Europarliamentarian Jacob von Weizsäcker (SPD), who as early as 2011 proposed what were essentially eurobonds.

4. Angela Merkel, speech on television, 18 March 2020; Mark Rutte, press conference, 12 March 2020; Emmanuel Macron, "Addresse aux Français", 13 April 2020.

5. Hannah Arendt, *The Human Condition* (Chicago, IL: University of Chicago Press, 2008 [1958]), 245.

6. See *Alarums & Excursions*, 21–61 (ch. 1).

7. Krastev, *Is it Tomorrow Yet?*, 54.

8. For an analysis of this speech and the furious reactions, see Werner Mussler, "Dijsselbloem, 'Ich bedauere, dass es als "Nord" gegen "Süd" aufgefasst wurde'", *Frankfurter Allgemeine Zeitung*, 22 March 2017.

9. Article by Heiko Maas, Federal Minister of Foreign Affairs, and Olaf Scholz, Federal Minister of Finance, "A response to the corona crisis in Europe based on solidarity", published on 6 April 2020 in different language versions in *Les Echos* (France),

La Stampa (Italy), *El País* (Spain), *Público* (Portugal) and *Ta Nea* (Greece).

10. See Jürgen Habermas, *The Structural Transformation of the Public Sphere: An Inquiry into a Category of Bourgeois Society*, trans. Thomas Burger and Frederick Lawrence (Cambridge: Polity, 1989). (Originally published as *Strukturwandel der Öffentlichkeit. Untersuchungen zu einer Kategorie der bürgerlichen Gesellschaft*, Berlin: Suhrkamp, 1962.)

11. Three astute twentieth-century thinkers recall, each in their own way, the range and power of this "public life". Apart from the already mentioned John Dewey and his *The Public and its Problems*, I am thinking of Hannah Arendt, *The Human Condition*, especially chapters 7, 27 and 28, and the dark Nazi ideologue Carl Schmitt, *Verfassungslehre* (Berlin: Duncker & Humblot, 1928), 243–4.

12. Michael Huether *et al.*, "Europa muss jetzt finanziell zusammenstehen", *Frankfurter Allgemeine Zeitung*, 21 March 2020.

13. Image borrowed from Mathieu Segers, "Europa's grote draai. Corona: hoe komen we uit de vertrouwenscrisis", *De Groene Amsterdammer*, 15 April 2020.

14. Bernardo de Miguel and Carlos E. Cué, "'Do we have a deal, Pedro?': an inside look at the clash at EU coronavirus summit", *El País*, 28 March 2020.

15. In his sound thesis "Membership of the European Council in a Historical and Constitutional Practice" (Zutphen: Europa Law Publishing, 2020) David Nederlof shows how French president Valéry Giscard d'Estaing and German chancellor Helmut Schmidt self-consciously began addressing each other as "member of the European Council" right after the institution was set up in early 1975, and immediately used the body as a stage for joint action. Almost all their successors, with famous pairs Mitterrand–Kohl, Sarkozy–Merkel and now Macron–Merkel, have done the same.

16. European Commission, "European Governance. A White Paper", 25 July 2001.

17. Jos de Beus, "The European Union as a community: an argument about the public sphere in international society and politics", in Paul van Seters (ed.), *Communitarianism in Law and Society*, (Lanham, MD: Rowman & Littlefield, 2006), 71–108, esp. 76.

18. For a more extensive analysis see Van Middelaar, *Alarums and Excursions*, ch. 7.

19. Peter Mair, "Government and Opposition in the European Union" (2007), referring to Otto Kirchheimer, "The waning of opposition in parliamentary regimes", *Social Research* 24 (1957), 129–56.

20. Based on the analysis of witnesses and experts cited in Claire Gatinois and Nicolas Ruisseau, "En Biélorussie, la révolution des femmes ébranle le pouvoir", *Le Monde*, 31 July 2020 and James Shotter and Max Seddon, "Protests break out in wake of Belarus presidential vote", *Financial Times*, 10 August 2020. See also n.n., "Weißrussland: Machthaber Lukaschenko räumt Covid-19-Erkrankung ein", *Der Spiegel*, 28 July 2020.

21. Lorenzo Marsili and Ulrike Guérot, "Elites have failed us. It is time to create a European republic", *The Guardian*, 10 May 2020. The former is the author (with Niccolò Milanese) of the book *Citizens of Nowhere: How Europe Can be Saved from Itself* (London: Zed Books, 2018), the latter of books including *Warum Europa eine Republik werden muss! Eine politische Utopie* (Bonn: Dietz, 2016).

5   GEOPOLITICS: BETWEEN CHINA AND THE UNITED STATES

1. Mission of the People's Republic of China to the European Union, "President Xi Jinping had a phone call with US President Donald Trump", 7 February 2020.

2. Bob Woodward, *Rage* (New York: Simon & Schuster, 2020), 19.

3. Woodward, *Rage*, 13.

4. Natasha Korecki, Alex Isenstadt, Anita Kumar *et al.*, "Inside Donald Trump's 2020 undoing", Politico.com, 7 November 2020.

5. European Commission, press release 6 April 2020, "Coronavirus: Chinese aid to the EU delivered to Italy"; the press service used this message of thanks as a reminder of the 56 tonnes of emergency aid that went in the other direction in February.

6. See prologue, page 4, text to endnote 9.

7. Mikko Huotari, head of the Mercator Institute of China Studies (MERICS), cited in Stuart Lau, "Coronavirus: Germany rejected 'China's bid for positive spin' on pandemic response", *South China Morning Post*, 27 April 2020.

8. For the conclusion that China had entered European public consciousness in a major crisis for the first time, see also the report by the European think tank Network on China (ETNC), *Covid-19 and Europe-China relations*, April 2020,

with contributions from almost 20 EU member states, and in particular John Seaman, "Introduction: China as partner, competitor and rival amid Covid-19", 5–10.

9. Fintan O'Toole, "Donald Trump has destroyed the country he promised to make great again", *Irish Times*, 25 April 2020.

10. Donald Trump, press conference 6 March 2020, cited in Edward Luce, "Trump and the great coronavirus meltdown", *Financial Times*, 16–17 May 2020.

11. In the terms used by secretary of state Mike Pompeo, "Communist China and the Free World's Future", a speech in the Richard Nixon Library and Museum, 23 July 2020, transcript and video available online.

12. Stuart Lau, "EU toned down report on Chinese disinformation after Beijing threatened 'repercussions', diplomatic sources say", *South China Morning Post*, 25 April 2020.

13. Pete Hoekstra, https://twitter.com/usambnl/status/ 1255466531733078018?s=20.

14. Josep Borrell, cited in Matt Apuzzo, "Top EU diplomat says disinformation report was not watered down for China", *New York Times*, 30 April 2020.

15. Conclusions of the European Council, 1–2 October, point 3. Macron, who earlier launched the term "sovereignty", has meanwhile recognized that the bar was set too high and endorsed "strategic autonomy". See interview on website *Le Grand Continent*, 16 November 2020.

16. Passage derived from AIV advice to the Dutch government, *China and the Strategic Task of the Netherlands in Europe*, June 2019, 8–12. The author is one of the compilers of the advice.

17. Angela Merkel, speech to the Munich Security Conference, 16 February 2019.

18. Geir Lundestad, "Empire by invitation? The United States and Western Europe, 1945–1952", *Journal of Peace Research* 23:3 (1986), 263–77.

19. Mark T. Esper, "Secretary of Defense readiness remarks at Heritage Foundation", 15 October 2020, available online.

20. Antony J. Blinken and Robert Kagan, "'America First' is only making the world worse. Here's a better approach", *Washington Post*, 1 January 2019.

21. European Commission and the High Representative of the Union for Foreign Affairs and Security Policy, "A new EU–US agenda for global change. Joint Communication to the European

Parliament, the European Council and the Council", 2 December 2020, available online. Conclusions of the European Council of 10–11 December 2020, point 29.

22. Kribbe, *The Strongmen*.

23. These notions have been elaborated more fully in the author's 2021 guest lectures at the Collège de France, forthcoming as *Le Réveil géopolitique de l'Europe* (Paris: Éditions du Collège de France, 2022).

24. See Annegret Kramp-Karrenbauer, "Europe still needs America", Politico.eu, 2 November 2020.

Index